HIDDEN
TREASURES

To Monica
Enjoy

Steven Maulert

HIDDEN
TREASURES

GWEN MOULIERT

TATE PUBLISHING
AND **ENTERPRISES**, LLC

This book is designed to provide accurate and authoritative information with regard to the subject matter covered. This information is given with the understanding that neither the author nor Tate Publishing, LLC is engaged in rendering legal, professional advice. Since the details of your situation are fact dependent, you should additionally seek the services of a competent professional.

The opinions expressed by the author are not necessarily those of Tate Publishing, LLC.

Published by Tate Publishing & Enterprises, LLC
127 E. Trade Center Terrace | Mustang, Oklahoma 73064 USA
1.888.361.9473 | www.tatepublishing.com

Tate Publishing is committed to excellence in the publishing industry. The company reflects the philosophy established by the founders, based on Psalm 68:11,
"The Lord gave the word and great was the company of those who published it."

Book design copyright © 2016 by Tate Publishing, LLC. All rights reserved.
Cover design by Joshua Rafols
Interior design by Jomar Ouano

Published in the United States of America

ISBN: 978-1-68319-301-2
1. Religion / Christian Life / Spiritual Growth
2. Religion / Biblical Meditations / General
16.08.30

CONTENTS

Introduction 7

1 The Voice of the Lord 9

   The Written Word of God 11

   My Sheep Hear My Voice 16

   Pay Attention to Your Spirit 19

   God Speaks Through People 22

   Dreams and Visions 32

2 The Four Winds 37

   The North Wind 41

   The South Wind 44

   The East Wind 46

   The West Wind 48

3 Vessels of Honor 51

4 The Seven Sprinklings 65
   The First of Seven 71
   The Second Sprinkling 72
   The Third Sprinkling 73
   The Fourth Sprinkling 74
   The Fifth Sprinkling 76
   The Sixth Sprinkling 77
   Where is the Seventh Sprinkling? 77

5 Rx for Health 81

6 Standing for Our Children 95

7 Thorns in the Flesh are a Mess.................. 111

8 Living with a Limp 127

9 The Disguise of Deception 139

10 How to Be a Giant Killer........................... 155

INTRODUCTION

When I was child, I had many questions about the Lord, the Bible and the Church. It seemed that when I would ask some of these questions many times over, I would hear, "It's a mystery of the church."

Well, I wanted someone to solve the mystery for me. Why couldn't I get any answers? It was not until years later when, as an adult, I accepted Jesus as my savior and was born again of His spirit.

At the time of my salvation, my pastor wanted to give me a little paperback New Testament with all the words of Jesus in red. I thanked him but quickly gave the Bible back to him.

I tried to explain to him that I could not understand the Bible because it is a mystery. I think as a young girl I read too many Nancy Drew novels, and I also loved the Hardy Boys mysteries adventure books. But this book was so different.

The pastor almost had to force me to accept this Bible as his gift to me. He challenged me to just read a little every day beginning in the Gospel of Saint John. Well I was up for his challenge and read every day this little paperback Bible with pictures, and to my amazement and awe, I understood it.

Then in the book of Ephesians, I became undone when I found out the mystery could be explained. Look at this verse: "Whereby, when ye read, ye may understand my knowledge in the *mystery* of Christ" (Eph. 3:4; emphasis added).

What I will be sharing in this book is over thirty years of mysteries that God's Spirit has given me on understanding as I have read His word.

Open your heart and spirit for new insights into old truths with great explanation as we open the hidden treasures and find nuggets of gold.

He said to them, "Therefore every teacher of the law who has been instructed about the kingdom of heaven is like the owner of a house who brings out of his storeroom *new treasures as well as old*" (Matthew 13:52; emphasis added).

Join me now on one of the most exciting treasure hunts you will ever be on. Blessings in Jesus.

1

THE VOICE OF THE LORD

The very first thing we need to address as you start to read this book is that no matter how spiritual or anointed or even prophetic an author is, only the word of God is infallible. What am I saying? That no matter how hard I try to keep my traditions from affecting this book, I am human and that's why the very first chapter will enable you to discover and discern my voice from the voice of the Lord.

I want to start with what happened to me when I was a very young Christian. I was involved with a wonderful women's ministry; however, all the women in this ministry were seasoned saints, and I was a novice. They would talk about the voice of the Lord as if he held conversations with them daily.

We then attended a conference with thousands of women, and the keynote speaker featured a tape for sale that she had ministered on, *How to Hear the Voice of God*. I would have paid anything to get my hands on that tape because I so desperately wanted to hear God's voice for myself.

As soon as I arrived home, one of the first things I did was set time aside to listen to this teaching without interruption. This happened to be a ninety-minute cassette, so therefore, with a soft couch and a hot cup of coffee, I ventured to hear His voice. After listening to this teaching, I decided I needed to hear it again. I wanted to make sure I did everything right according to directions, so after three hours, I felt as if I was ready to approach God and have Him speak to me.

I need to mention I was informed that there are three voices that speak to us on a daily basis: there is the voice of our own human spirit, the voice of the Holy Spirit, and the voice of Satan, or if you prefer, an evil spirit. So the greatest question I now had was how do I tell the difference?

Thank God for this woman's teaching ministry because the tape came with some practical instructions. First, I was to silence the voice of self (sorry to say I haven't learned how to do that to this day), then I was to bind the voice of all evil spirits; now the only voice left to come to me would be the voice of the Lord. Sounds great, doesn't it? So upstairs I went to tell myself to shut up, to bind up all the voices of the wicked one, and to listen for His voice.

I knelt by my bed with my eyes closed and my hands together in the prayer position. I did all that I have learned from the message. After I silenced myself and Satan, I said, "Speak, Lord, your servant listens."

As clear as anything I have ever heard with my inner voice, I heard Romans 18:8. I was ecstatic! Oh my! God had spoken to me! I ran down the stairs with tears flowing down my cheeks to get my hands on a Bible so I can know what God was saying to me. I thought, *quick, Gwen, find the book of Romans.* I finally got to Romans, and I can't believe what I saw. There were only sixteen chapters in that book.

I was heartbroken but then I began to laugh. I was sure that even the angels found some joy in my sincerity, but I soon realized this was not the way for me to hear from God.

So I began my search for how to hear His voice. God speaks in many ways to us today. I want to share five that have been very helpful to me over the years.

The Written Word of God

There are some wonderful examples of God speaking to people in the Old Testament as well as the New Testament. In fact, in the book of Hebrews, we see how God spoke in days gone by. Hebrews 1:1–2 in the NIV version says, "In the past God spoke to our forefathers through the prophets at many times and in various ways but in these last days he has spoken to us by his Son whom he appointed heir of all things and through whom he made the universe."

The Bible tells us in the Old Testament he spoke in various or many different ways, and he spoke through the prophets. There is one prophet in particular that he spoke to when this prophet was only a young man. I am sure you have heard of him. His name is Samuel, and his story is found in 1 Samuel.

His mother's name was Hannah, and she could not have children because the Lord had closed up her womb, and she was barren. Her husband's name was Elkanah, and he had another wife named Peninnah with whom he had children, so it was clear that this infertility was Hannah's problem. She prayed and prayed for a child. The pain was almost unbearable, she could not eat, she was crying, and so she went into the house of God to pour out her soul.

She made what is now a famous promise that if God would give her a son, she would give him to the Lord for all the days of his life. Well, God answered this prayer and opened her womb, and she became pregnant. She named their son Samuel; his name means "the Lord has heard me."

He was a much-wanted child who was born as a direct answer to a prayer. When he was about three, his mother took him to the temple and fulfilled her vow. She gave him over to the Lord's service under the care of Eli the priest.

A Child with a Heart for Ministry

There are some awesome things written about Samuel when he was just a small child. Let's look at three of them. His mother has now left him at the temple in Shiloh, and the first thing the Bible says about him is found in 1 Samuel 1:28: "Therefore also I have lent him to the LORD; as long as he liveth he shall be lent to the LORD. And he worshipped the LORD there."

Even though he is a young boy, *he is a worshipper*. Isn't that a wonderful thing to see, a child worships God? The second thing written about him is in 1 Samuel 2:18: "But Samuel ministered before the LORD, being a child, girded with a linen ephod." Not only did Samuel worship, but he *ministered* or served, if you will, with a linen ephod. To wear such a garment was really an honor, for the ephod was a holy garment worn by the priest and by a king. (Nice to know we are now kings and priests!) We see Samuel the worshipper and Samuel the minister. Now let us look at the third and final thing written about him before the voice of God comes to him.

The final thing I want to share with you is found in 1 Samuel 2:26: "And the child Samuel grew in stature and was *in favor* both *with the* LORD and also with men" (emphasis added). Here we see him as a worshipper, a minister, and a young man who has favor with God and man. What more could we want for our children than these three things? This last verse—favor with the Lord and men—was quoted about Jesus in Luke 2:52: "And Jesus grew in wisdom and *stature and in favor with God and man*" (emphasis added).

So what have we established thus far? That Samuel was raised in a godly home and was an answer to a prayer. He was even raised in the church his whole childhood. We would assume that if anyone would hear God's voice it would be Samuel. Yet when the Lord spoke to him, he did not recognize His voice and ran to his mentor.

The biblical account is in 1 Samuel 3: God calls him, and he runs to Eli the priest and asks "did you call me?" The priest tells him to return to his bed, and once again the Lord speaks. Then Samuel goes to Eli again, and then the Bible says something quite startling in 1 Samuel 3:7: "Now Samuel did not yet know the LORD, neither was the word of the Lord yet revealed unto him."

How Could He Miss God's Voice?

Did you read this right? Samuel did not know the Lord. A worshipper, a minister, and a young man who possessed favor, however, when the Lord spoke, he missed it. How is it he didn't know the Lord? Because the word of the Lord had not been revealed to him yet! We know God, and we know His voice through His word. Hebrews 1:2 says that God speaks to us today through his son. His son is the word of God: "In the beginning was the Word, and the Word was with God, and the Word was God. The same was in the beginning with God. And the Word was made flesh and dwelt among us and we beheld his glory, the glory as of the only begotten of the Father, full of grace and truth" (1 John 1:1–2).

So here is my conclusion of this story: if Samuel can miss or misinterpret the voice of God, so can we. That is why the number one way to discern the voice of the Lord is through his word, the Bible.

The story is not over for Samuel. God revealed his word and himself to this prophet and look at the outcome found in 1 Samuel 3:19–21: "The LORD was with him and did let none of his words fall to the ground. And all Israel from Dan even to Beersheba knew that Samuel was established to be a prophet of the LORD. And the Lord appeared again in Shiloh: for the LORD revealed himself to Samuel in Shiloh by the word of the LORD."

Not one word from Samuel fell to the ground, and God continued to speak to him and direct his thoughts the rest of his life. He became a great prophet; he anointed King David and was himself a great intercessor for the people of God.

The number one way to hear God's voice is to read his word. Let's take a moment and talk about the second way to hear Him. After you know the written word, it is safe to listen for the spoken word from God.

There are many things in our lives that we want God's direction, and yet we cannot find a scripture that addresses that issue. For example, I never read in the Bible where I was to marry a plumber, but I did. When I have been invited to speak and minister, I have not found in the Bible the different states I have traveled to. So there is not only the written word of God but the spoken word from God. This is the second way to hear his voice. What about the college for your child, the location you are to live in, or the career you are to advance in? In all of these important decisions, we would want the guidance of God.

My Sheep Hear My Voice

Jesus said we would know his voice; in addition, we would recognize him over the voice of a stranger (John 10:1–5). Let's look for a minute at the spoken word of God. For our case example, we will use Elijah. Let me tell you the short story form of the past events. He exposed the worship of idols, he was able to call down fire from heaven, and the people chose to serve Jehovah. He killed all the false prophets of Baal, and when word reached the queen mother Jezebel, she put out a death threat against the servant of God.

It amazes me that he could confront a nation, call down fire, kill false prophets, yet, this one wicked woman made him run for his life in fear. In 1 Kings 19, he was severely depressed; when an angel woke him and told him to eat and to rest, he was then sent to Mount Horeb because God wanted to speak to him. At Mount Horeb, he entered a cave, and the Lord spoke.

Spectacular or Supernatural?

> And he said, Go forth and stand upon the mount before the LORD. And behold, the LORD passed by and a great and strong wind rent the mountains and brake in pieces the rocks before the LORD. But the

> LORD was not in the wind and after the wind an earthquake but the LORD was not in the earthquake and after the earthquake a fire but the LORD was not in the fire and after the fire a still small voice. (1 Kings 19:11–12)

Notice with me that the voice of the Lord was not in the wind, nor was his voice in the earthquake or the fire. What makes this so unusual is that these three ways were how God spoke in the Old Testament. In the book of Job, the first time God spoke, he did in a whirl*wind*. When he gave the law to Moses, he spoke by an *earthquake*, and only days before, he spoke to Elijah through the *fire* and to Moses in the burning bush. So what am I saying? If we always look for something spectacular—earthquakes, flames of fire, or whirlwinds—we could miss the small whisper. How did God speak in a still small voice or, as other versions put it, a whisper?

Always remember that the spoken word must line up with the written word. That is why it is so important to read our Bibles. Back in the '80s, I wrote my first book, which was my testimony, and I sent the manuscript to several publishers. I became very discouraged as one by one my new book was rejected. I thought okay, I would try one more time, so I sent my book to another publisher. They were kind enough to call and say it would be six to eight weeks before they could evaluate the manuscript. At that time, I felt like six to eight weeks was a lifetime; I knew I had to let it go and trust God.

UPS at Their Best

One evening, I was reading my Bible, and I got to Psalm 112:7: "He shall not be afraid of evil tidings; his heart is fixed trusting in the Lord." Here was the written word, and in my spirit I heard the spoken word: God told me the book would be returned tomorrow. So, in essence, another rejection was on the way, but I was to fix my heart and trust in the Lord.

In where I live, we didn't have mail delivery, so I drove about four miles each day to pick up my mail. As I pondered the scripture and the whisper, I realized I wasn't prepared for another rejection, so I decided not to pick up my mail the next day. Now I would have another twenty-four hours to get my heart fixed on trusting in the Lord, and I would not fear the evil tidings.

The next day when my children arrived home from school, we left for the mall to do some shopping. When we came back home and I pulled my car into the driveway, there sat a brown manila envelope on my front porch courtesy of United Parcel Service or better known as UPS. Just as the Lord has said the book would be returned tomorrow, I picked up the envelope and got overwhelmed with joy, not because there was another rejection, but because I heard the voice of God.

Whenever God speaks to us, it should be overwhelming; after all, what is man that he is mindful of him. I thought about God being the creator, the all-powerful, holy one; and tears flowed in praise to a God who would take the time to speak to a homemaker who lived in Pomona, New Jersey.

Just an update, my testimony was published, and the title is *Hyper to Holy–How God Touched a Housewife.*

Pay Attention to Your Spirit

Thus, the number one way to hear his voice is through his written word, and next through his spoken word. But there is another way God speaks to us without really saying anything; we will call this third way the inner witness.

Have you ever had a strong impression about something or someone? It seems all of a sudden they're in your heart. You call them or pray for them and find that this truly was the leading of the Lord. The Bible addresses this with scriptures that I missed for years. Let us look at the inner witness of the Holy Spirit as he guides us.

Before we open the verses in Acts, I think it is important to share a verse from Daniel that helps us understand where we would sense the leading of the spirit: "I was grieved in my spirit in the midst of my body and the visions of my head troubled me" (Daniel 7:15). Did you see it? He said that when his spirit was grieved, it was in the middle of his body, the belly area: "The spirit of man is the candle of the

Lord, searching all the inward parts of the belly" (Proverbs 20:27).

It is clear from the verses that the Spirit of God is in the inward part of our belly or, as Daniel said, the middle of our bodies. Too many times, we think all the direction will come to our head first, but most times it starts in the heart.

"Now when they had gone throughout Phrygia and the region of Galatia and were forbidden of the Holy Ghost to preach the word in Asia, after they were come to Mysia, they assayed to go into Bithynia but the Spirit suffered them not and they passing by Mysia came down to Troas" (Acts 16:6–8).

Forbidden by the Spirit

I would have never thought that the Holy Spirit would forbid anyone to preach, but the Bible is very clear that on their way to Asia to preach, the Holy Spirit stopped Paul and Silas. Before we go any deeper on this text, please understand that timing is so important—this was not the time for them to minister in Asia. In Acts 19, when the time was right, they preached to all of Asia for over two years (Acts 19:10).

How did the spirit forbid Paul from going to Asia? First, the word *forbid* means to prevent or to hinder from the *Strong's Concordance*. The dictionary gives this definition: "an order not to do something, make something impossible, to prohibit."

Then they decided to go to Mysia or to Bithynia, and the Spirit suffered them not. I think we need this in the Amplified Bible: "And when they had come opposite Mysia, they tried to go into Bithynia, but the Spirit of Jesus did not permit them."

This is when you sense in your spirit something God is telling you. There may be no words involved but a sense of grieving or disturbance. Please obey and pray! How precious these scriptures are to me now, but it was not always so.

A good number of years ago, I was asked to go to Texas for a convention. When I shared this with my best friend and traveling companion, she said she didn't want to go this time and was I sure this was the will of God for me.

I made plans to go without her, and I must be honest that because I really wanted to go, I did not heed her counsel, and I really didn't pray. Off I went to Texas! The day before I was to leave, I got the hives. And by the time my husband came home from work, I was a mass of red raised bumps. I got more and more nervous, and the hives began to spread.

I could not sleep. Thank God for a godly husband, he and I began to pray. I was not going to allow the devil to stop me, so we spent a long time in prayer and spiritual warfare. The only problem was we were going in the wrong direction.

We prayed until the wee hours of the morning around 3:00 a.m. I was having trouble breathing, so we went to the emergency room. They gave me several injections and told me to go home and begin bed rest. Bed rest? I was on my way to Texas! I went home and packed, and we then went to the airport.

Once in Texas, I expected the hives would leave because I thought I was in obedience to God's call in my life to minister his word. Little did I know back then about the inner witness and the timing of God.

I was ill for the whole ten days I was in Texas; in fact, I had to be taken to the hospital twice. Finally, I arrived home and was very discouraged because I could not seem to obtain my healing. Once safe at home, I began to cry out to the Lord (which I should have done days ago), trying to understand why this affliction continued. Here I was teaching healing, and I am not well.

Finally, I asked the $64,000 question—why? Sure enough, the Lord answered me; He said, "I told you not to go to Texas." I then, and only then, realized that he had indeed spoken through the inner witness because deep down I knew something was not right, and I chose to ignore it. He had spoken to me through my travel partner as well as my husband who both wanted me to reconsider the trip once I got sick.

God Speaks Through People

The fourth way he speaks to us today is through others. Let's use a familiar Bible character, and what a character he was—I am speaking of Peter. God used him in a very powerful way to bring the gospel to the gentiles. If you want the whole story with details, just read Acts chapter 10. To make a long story short, the Jews didn't fellowship with non-Jews. God showed Peter through a vision that he was to enter the home of a Gentile.

Peter obeyed God and went to the home of a man named Cornelius, who had all his family and friends awaiting Peter's arrival. When Peter was telling the story of Jesus, something miraculous happened: these folks all got saved and spirit-filled and spoke in other tongues. Peter was stunned along with his Jewish traveling companions. There was no denying their salvation; in fact, Peter said since God gave these Gentiles the same gift he gave us, let's get them water baptized.

The truth in this story is not that God decided to save the non-Jews, but that God showed Peter he is no respecter of persons. Peter said it best in Acts 10:34: "Then Peter opened his mouth and said of a truth I perceived that God is no respecter of persons." This was the lesson Peter was to learn.

Nevertheless, just like so many of us, we can forget the lessons of life. After many years had gone by, Peter acted in a way that was inappropriate: He was in Antioch where he spent time with the Gentiles, but when the Jewish believers would come there, he withdrew himself.

God then sent the apostle Paul to confront him.

> But when Peter was come to Antioch I withstood him to the face because he was to be blamed. For

before that certain came from James he did eat with the Gentiles but when they were come, he withdrew and separated himself fearing them which were of the circumcision. And the other Jews dissembled likewise with him; insomuch that Barnabas also was carried away with their dissimulation. But when I saw that they walked not uprightly according to the truth of the gospel, I said unto Peter before them all, if thou, being a Jew livest after the manner of Gentiles and not as do the Jews, why compellest thou the Gentiles to live as do the Jews? (Galatians 2:11–15, KJV)

This is only one example. Now how about Nathan speaking to David in 2 Samuel 12:1? There are many examples of prophets speaking to the kings and the people as the voice of God.

Gifts, Signs, and Wonders

I wanted to keep this teaching in order of significance: always the Bible first and foremost, then the spoken word, the inner witness, other people, and I now want to share about the gifts of the Spirit.

The gifts of the Holy Spirit are listed in 1 Corinthians chapter 12. It is of note that there are nine gifts of the Spirit and nine fruits of the Spirit. Please, God, help us stay balanced. God does use his gifts to speak to his people.

Of the nine gifts or manifestations of the spirit, they can be easily divided into three sets of three. Let me list them as the Bible does, then we will do the division.

> For to one is given by the Spirit the word of wisdom; to another the word of knowledge by the same Spirit; to another faith by the same Spirit; to another the gifts of healing by the same Spirit; to another the working of miracles; to another prophecy; to another discerning of spirits; to another divers kinds of tongues; to another the interpretation of tongues: But all these worketh that one and the selfsame Spirit, dividing to every man severally as he will. (1 Corinthians 12:8–11, King James Version)

The word of wisdom, word of knowledge, then faith and gifts of healing, followed by miracles, prophecy, discerning of spirits, and finally the gifts of tongues with the accompanying of interpretation.

Three gifts do something; they are miracles, faith, and healings. Three gifts reveal something; they are discerning of spirits, word of wisdom, and the word of knowledge. The final three gifts say something; they are tongues and interpretation along with prophecy. Of these vocal gifts, the Lord can indeed speak to you. He can also use the three gifts that reveal.

A Personal Word from the Lord

I believe we need to be careful when we seek to hear God's voice through the gifts of the spirit. Why is that? Because whenever a person is involved, there can be human error. In the book of Jeremiah as well as the book of Ezekiel, we are warned about prophets who say they are speaking from God; however, it's their own human spirit.

I have given a definition to the word *prophecy* that has helped countless people to understand why we are told to judge the words of prophecy (1 Cor. 14:29). Now remember this is just my definition. I believe that prophecy is the merging of the divine through a human vessel. If prophecy was always 100 percent God, He would never tell us to judge it. Who are we to ever judge God? He is perfect; however, his children are not so perfect. Let me get back to the word of God from Ezekiel 13:3: "Thus saith the Lord GOD, Woe unto the foolish prophets that follow their own spirit and have seen nothing."

It is clear from this verse that there have been prophets who follow their own human spirit. Jeremiah deals in detail with this problem. Look with me at Jeremiah 14:14: "And the Lord said to me, 'The prophets prophesy lies in My name. I have not sent them, commanded them, nor spoken to them; they prophesy to you a false vision, divination, a worthless thing and the deceit of their heart'" (NKJV). I hope you did not miss the last phrase of this verse, "the deceit of their heart." The Amplified Bible says the deceit of their own minds. The New International Version says delusions of their minds. Before we move to the genuine, let me define the words used in these verses, words like *deceit* and *delusion*.

The Bible says that the heart is deceitfully wicked, and who can know it? (Jer. 17:9). Therefore, we need to be *cautious without being critical*. The definition of the word *deceit* is a dishonest practice, the act of misleading someone; and the thesaurus uses words like *trickery*, *pretense*, or *sham*. By definition, the word *delusion* means a false belief or a mistaken notion; and again, the thesaurus uses the terms *illusion*, *fantasy*, or *figment of the imagination*.

The Real McCoy

I want to share a time when I heard the voice of God through the gifts of the spirit. It was April 1990, and I was hosting a women's retreat in Ocean City, New Jersey. I was in the hotel lobby greeting the women as they entered, when a woman named Cathy approached me. Cathy said that she had been praying for me and believed she had a word from the Lord for me. What she said next was a complete shock to me: "I the Lord have changed your heart. I am calling you into full-time ministry, and you are to be a pastor." What did she say?

To be honest with you, I did not believe her word, nor did I think that she was speaking to me from God. I dismissed it and got involved with the work at hand for this retreat. Everything went beautifully through Friday evening and Saturday morning. Then it happened: God confirmed his word through another person. We had decided to have an anointing service that Saturday night, so before we began to anoint the attendees, we had asked a pastor to come forward and anoint us with oil as we prepared to anoint the women. As the pastor put the oil in my forehead, these were the exact words we all heard, "I the Lord have changed your heart. I have called you and your husband to pastor and to be in full-time ministry."

When I heard the words, I fell to the ground sobbing. There was no way for me to deny I heard from the Lord. As I was on the floor crying, Cathy jumped up from her seat and ran to the front of the room saying, "I heard from God, I heard from God!" Well, Cathy, so did I! After I got myself composed, we had an awesome move of God as we anointed and prayed with each person.

The retreat ended Sunday morning, and I headed home. It was not until I was home and alone that I began to process the word I received. Why, if God had a word for me, did he have to tell two strangers and not me, his daughter? I was perplexed and a little confused at the time; I had always taught that when the gifts of the Spirit, such as prophecy or words of knowledge, were in operation, it would confirm what was already in your heart. Well, let me tell you this word—being a pastor was nowhere in my heart!

My husband had a great job as a union plumber for over twenty years, and nowhere did we plan to start a new adventure like this in our late forties. The first thing I did was tell my husband all about what happened to me that weekend, and he in turn told me that he believed he was called to be a pastor, and he had a word of prophecy over eleven years ago! All the time, he had been standing on and waiting for God to tell him when it would be fulfilled.

A Women Pastor: I Do Not Think So!

Early in the morning, I got up to spend time with the Lord, and I just started to cry. I asked him that if you wanted me to be a pastor, why didn't you tell me? I knew in a moment the answer. I did not believe that a woman should be a pastor, therefore, I would have never heard God's voice on such an issue as this.

What was I to do? My tradition and upbringing made it clear to me that to be a minister, you must be a male. How true it is what Jesus said in Mark 7:13, "Making the word of God of none effect through your tradition which ye have delivered: and many such like things do ye." My tradition had made God's word to no effect. Look at how this reads in the Amplified Bible: "Thus you are nullifying and making void and of no affect through your tradition, which you [in turn] hand on." I did not know I was making the Bible void because I was holding on to the traditions I had learned as a child. What was I to do?

I decided to study all the scriptures about women in the Bible; if I was going to read any books on the subject of women in ministry, I made sure men wrote them. I did not want to acquire a rebellious spirit, so I set to find out what God said about women, not what people say God said—

there is a vast difference. I studied all the verses I could find about women, equality, submission, my role, and on and on the list could go.

For over two years, I delved into this subject with a passion for truth. I was not trying to prove anything to anyone; I just wanted to understand the call of God on my life. Then I went to a conference in Texas and the guest speaker was Dr. Fuchsia Pickett. There were over ten thousand women in the coliseum. She ministered the word beautifully, and I was held captive by her every word. And then she said something that hit me like a ton of bricks.

Her Name is Adam

Dr. Pickett's statement was that God did not create Adam and Eve, but just Adam! She said Eve did not get her name until after the Fall, when Adam named her Eve. We went to the Bible and sure enough in Genesis 5:1 is the generations of Adam: "In the day that God created man in the likeness of God made he him: male and female created he them and blessed them and *called their name Adam* in the day when they were created" (emphasis added).

Look at Genesis 3:20, after the Fall and the curse, Adam then names his wife Eve: "And Adam called his wife's name Eve; because she was the mother of all the living." God named her Adam when they were first created in the garden, and they were equal.

Now that the last Adam has come, we go back to our state before the Fall—men and women are equal. How much this helped me understand the book of Romans, when Adam is blamed over and over again for the actions of his wife. When it speaks of Adam from the garden before sin, that was her name as well.

Even the New Testament makes this clear in Galatians 3:26–29:

> For ye are all the children of God by faith in Christ Jesus. For as many of you as have been baptized into Christ have put on Christ. There is neither Jew nor Greek, there is neither bond nor free, there is *neither male nor female*: for ye are all one in Christ Jesus. And if ye be Christ's then are ye Abraham's seed and heirs according to the promise. (emphasis added)

While at the conference, I jumped up and shouted; people must have thought I had lost my mind! In fact, I had lost my tradition of men, and now I knew God's word would be active, alive, and effective in this new calling He had put in my life.

So we obeyed his call, and two years later, we opened our church. It's been over twenty-three years now and God has poured out his blessings on us. My husband left his trade, and by faith we followed the leading of God. I have never once regretted our obedience and how thankful I am that God's words set me free.

Dreams and Visions

So far, we have seen a number of ways to hear God's voice. I wanted to keep dreams and visions in the last place in this chapter. Dreams and visions can come without it being from God, and it takes maturity and discernment to know when you have heard from God in this manner. The Bible has many examples of men and women receiving direction from God through a dream or a vision.

When it comes to visions, they are plentiful in the Bible: Joseph had three dreams concerning his pending marriage to Mary to take baby Jesus to Egypt and when to return home. Jacob had a vision; we call it Jacobs's ladder. Isaiah had a vision of the holiness of God. Daniel had visions. Ezekiel as well. And in the New Testament, Ananias, Cornelius, Peter, Paul, and John the Revelator all had visions from God.

Just as God can give dreams and vision, so can other influences. I am reminded of the dreams of Nebuchadnezzar in the book of Daniel when he builds an idol of himself and wanted all the people to bow in worship to this statue. We know of three young Hebrew men who obeyed God, knowing that Nebuchadnezzar's dreams were not from God because they were instructed to bow and worship only the one true God Jehovah.

However, we are told in the book of Acts that dreams and visions would be genuine and would increase in the last days. Let us look at the prophetic promise that we are seeing being fulfilled in our days. "But this is that which was spoken by the prophet Joel: 'And it shall come to pass in the last days saith God, I will pour out of my Spirit upon all flesh and your sons and your daughters shall prophesy and your young men shall see visions and your old men shall dream'" (Acts 2:16–17).

The word of warning is to make sure that if you have a dream or a vision, it lines up with the word of God and that you are not disturbed in your spirit. Job had some dreams that he thought were from God. He even says in Job 7:14, "Then thou scarest me with dreams and terrifiest me through visions." Later, Job found out that it was not God who did this to him but the devil. So please be careful in this arena.

How Do I Judge What Voice I am Hearing?

Since there are three voices we contend with—self, Satan, and our savior—how do we judge? I have found one portion of scripture very helpful:

> Let the prophets speak two or three and let the other judge. If any thing be revealed to another that sitteth by let the first hold his peace for ye may all prophesy one by one, that all may learn and all may be comforted. The spirits of the prophets are subject to the prophets for God is not the author of confusion but of peace. (1 Corinthians 14:29–33)

Peace or Confusion?

The verses in 1 Corinthians are dealing with how to judge a prophecy. I will have to save that teaching for another book. Nevertheless, this is dealing with someone speaking as a prophet and how they can speak one at a time. The real crux of the matter is found in verse 33: it tells us that God is the author of peace, not confusion.

Whenever I think I have heard from the Lord, the first thing I do is check to see if I am now confused or do I have peace. I am not talking necessarily about peace of mind but peace of heart. You can have God speak something to you that might be a struggle, yet, deep in your heart or soul or spirit, there is a great sense of peace.

My husband has the gift of giving, and I remember one time I came home from a meeting, and he told me the Lord had spoken to him. I said, "And how much will this cost me?" kidding around because I know his heart. Well, sure enough, the Lord did speak to him about sending a large gift to a ministry many states away. My head didn't want to do it, but I had tremendous peace in my heart.

Remember, the Bible said God is not the author of confusion. If a word confuses you, wait and pray. If it is the Lord, he will continue to make his will known to you. He can and does speak in many different ways.

I want to end this chapter with a cute e-mail that was sent to me titled "If God Had E-mail."

Thank you for calling Heaven. Please select one of the following options:

> Press 1 for Requests
> Press 2 for Thanksgiving
> Press 3 for Complaints
> Press 4 for all other inquiries

> I am sorry; all of our angels and saints are busy helping other sinners right now. However, your prayer is important to us and we will answer it in the order it was received. Please stay on the line. If you would like to speak to God,

> Press 1 for Jesus
> Press 2 for the Holy Spirit,
> Press 3 if you would like to hear King David sing a Psalm while you are holding,
> Press 4 to find a loved one that has been assigned to heaven then enter his or her Social Security number, followed by the pound sign.

> For reservations at heaven, please enter JOHN 3:16

> For answers to nagging questions about dinosaurs, the age of the earth, life on other planets, and where Noah's Ark is, please wait until you arrive.

> Our computers show that you have already prayed once today. Please hang up and try again tomorrow.

This office is now closed for the weekend to observe a religious holiday.

Please pray again on Monday after 9:30 am. If you are calling after hours and need emergency assistance, please contact your local Pastor.

How grateful I am that we can speak to the Lord any time, and he hears us. Not only does he hear us, he speaks to us. I pray that we will always have an ear to hear what the Spirit would say to us the church.

"The voice of the Lord is powerful; the voice of the Lord is full of majesty, the voice of the Lord divideth the flames of fire, the voice of the Lord shaketh the wilderness" (Psalm 29:4, 7).

2

THE FOUR WINDS

The word of God has a very important numerical system. I am sure you are aware of some of the common ones: the number *three* for the godhead, the number *five* for grace, the number *six* is the number of man, and the number *seven* is the number for God's completion.

The number *four* relates to the earth.

- Four directions: north, south, east, west
- Four seasons: summer, winter, fall, spring
- Four kinds of spiritual soil (Matthew 13)
- Four great earthly kingdoms (Daniel 7:3)
- Four horsemen of the tribulation (Revelation 6)
- Fourfold earthly ministry of Christ. In Matthew, Jesus is described as King, in Mark as a servant, in Luke as the perfect man, and in John as the mighty God.

In this chapter, we will look at the four winds of God. We need to understand about winds, what they stand for, and how to see God release his breath on each of us. We'll start by defining the word *wind*. In the Old Testament, it is the Hebrew word *ruwach* (roo'-akh) from the *Strong's Concordance*, for wind, breath, mind, spirit. It is the identical word used when we refer to the Spirit of God.

Look at Genesis 1:2: "In the beginning God created the heaven and the earth and the earth was without form, and void; and darkness was upon the face of the deep. And the *Spirit of God* moved upon the face of the waters" (emphasis added).

In the New Testament, it also refers to the Spirit of God or the Holy Spirit when we talk about the wind of God. I am, in essence, saying the Spirit of God or the breath of God is called the winds.

In Psalm 148:8, look at what the Lord says concerning the wind: "Fire and hail, snow and vapors; stormy wind fulfilling his word." In the Amplified Bible, it says that the stormy wind fulfill his orders. The New International Version says that the stormy wind does his bidding; now we can see that God uses his winds to accomplish his word or his orders of bidding.

There are many descriptions for the winds in the Bible; I just want to cover a few.

Come Thou Winds From His Treasures

Jeramiah 4:11 talks about a dry wind or a serene wind, and Ezekiel 13:11 mentions a stormy wind, which is the whirlwind. In Johah 1:14, we find the great wind (great in intensity), and in the New Testament book of Matthew 14:30, we see the boisterous or firm wind. When the Bible talks of the winds in conection with the Holy Spirit in Acts 2:2, it's a mighty or forcible wind, and in James 3:4, there is a fierce or stiff and harsh wind.

Where do these winds come from that fufill God's word? Psalms 135:7 tells us, "He causeth the vapors' to ascend from the ends of the earth; he maketh lightnings for the rain; he bringeth the *wind out of his treasuries*" (emphasis added). Jeremiah also confirms this truth in chapter 51 verse 16: "When he uttereth his voice, there is a multitude of waters in the heavens; and he causeth the vapors' to ascend from the ends of the earth: he maketh lightnings with rain, and bringeth forth the wind out of his *treasures*" (emphasis added).

Since God keeps the winds in his treasury, we need to find out what his treasures are. You will be very happy to learn that the word *treasuries* in Jeremiah 51:16 and Jeremiah 10:13 is the word *storehouse*. God's spirit or wind is kept in his storehouses, which are his treasuries. Hallelujah, the storehouse is the local assembly, church, or temple.

Winds of Heaven and Earth

I first started to study the winds of God when I was reading the book of Zechariah chapter 2. It was talking about a man with a measuring line going to Jerusalem to measure its length and breadth. Verse 5 was very exciting to me; it says "For I saith the Lord 'will be unto her a wall of fire roundabout and will be the glory in the midst of her.'" Wow, a wall of fire and glory in the middle. And then the next scripture riveted me: "Ho, ho come forth and flee from the land of the north saith the Lord for I have spread you abroad as the four winds of the heaven." Did you catch it? The four winds of heaven! This began the search, and I discovered that the Bible not only talks about the four winds of heaven, but it talks about the four winds of the earth.

In Revelation 7:1, it says, "And after these things I saw four angels standing on the four corners of the earth holding the four winds of the earth that the wind should not blow on the earth nor on the sea, nor on any tree." Now I noticed that there were four winds of earth and four winds of heaven. What could these four winds be?

As we look at the north, south, east, and west winds, my prayer is that you will be able to discover where you are at the present time and which wind God is blowing in your life. From the verse above, we see that the angels have control to hold back the wind. There will be another time when the angels will be involved with the four winds: In Jesus's words

But in those days, after that tribulation, the sun shall be darkened, and the moon shall not give her light, and the stars of heaven shall fall and the powers that are in heaven shall be shaken. And then shall they see the Son of man coming in the clouds with great power and glory. And then shall he send his angels, and shall gather together his elect from the four winds, from the uttermost part of the earth to the uttermost part of heaven. (Mark 13:24–27)

The angels will gather God's elect from the four winds in heaven and on the earth.

The North Wind

To make this study easy to understand, we will look at the four winds in this order: north, south, east, and west. Beginning with the north, we see Job had a lot to say on the winds of God. As a matter of fact, the first two winds, the north and south, are found in this book.

"Now men see not the bright light which is in the cloud: but the *wind* passeth and *cleanseth* them. Fair weather cometh out of *the north* with God is terrible majesty. Touching the Almighty, we cannot find him out: he is excellent in power and in judgment, and in plenty of justice: he will not afflict" (Job 37:21; emphasis added).

I want to look at this portion in several versions before I go into detail about the north wind. This scripture in the Amplified Bible says, "And now men cannot look upon the light when it is bright in the skies, when the wind has passed and cleared them. Golden brightness and splendor come out of the north; [if men can scarcely look upon it, how much less upon the] terrible splendor and majesty God has upon Himself."

The New International Version says, "Now no one can look at the sun, bright as it is in the skies after the wind has swept them clean. Out of the north he comes in golden splendor; God comes in awesome majesty."

I find it very interesting that the King James, Amplified, and the New International all say that this wind from the north is a cleansing wind. When the King James says fair weather comes from the north, it means to shimmer as gold. The north wind comes to cleanse, so we will be like gold. I like the above verse that he comes from the north as golden splendor or golden brightness. We are to reflect his image, his glory, and his splendor; and we cannot do so if we have not been cleansed.

As silly as it seems, when I decided to look up the word *north*, I remember as a young person how annoyed I would become when I couldn't spell something, and I would ask my mom or dad how to spell it, and they would tell me to look it up in the dictionary. Question for you: how can I look up something I cannot spell? Well, I can handle the word *north*; my fear was that all it would say is a direction to the north. I was in for quite a surprise from the *Hebrew Lexicon*—the word *north* is described as "hidden, dark, obscure."

It began to make sense to me now. I need the north wind of God to cleanse me from anything dark or hidden or obscured. There is no way I can shimmer as gold to reflect him if I have hidden areas in my life or heart that are dark.

After the Lord opened this north wind to me, I called for his wind of cleansing. I knew deep down that I still had areas of hidden dark things in my heart. God was faithful, and he showed me an area where as a child I had been sexually abused; for years I refused to acknowledge it due to hurt, pain, shame, and confusion.

I once heard a phrase that has helped me many times, "God heals what he reveals." I do not want to take the time now to share how his wind of cleansing blew through my heart and soul. But this first wind from the north cleansed me, and after the process of forgiveness had taken place, I did indeed shimmer, and I felt as priceless to the Lord as pure gold.

Don't fear what is hidden! God will cleanse us if we just ask him! Even Proverbs 20:9 shows us that we all have sins: "Who can say 'I have made my heart clean, I am pure from my sin?'" The problem is many times we have sins or issues we are not aware of. "Thou has set our iniquities before thee, our secret sins in the light of thy countenance" (Psalm 90:8). I want any secret sin exposed by his presence so he can cleanse me, and like the psalmist, this should be our prayer: "Create in me a clean heart, O God; and renew a right spirit within me" (Psalm 51:10).

The South Wind

In Psalm 78:26, God says, "He caused an east wind to blow in the heaven and by his power he brought in the south wind." In the book of Job, the north wind cleanses. Let's look at this book again and see what the Bible has to say on the south wind.

"How thy garments are warm when he quieteth the earth by the south wind?" (Job 37:17). When I read this verse, I think of how nice it feels to put on a warm garment. When we have snow and I am really cold, I will put a sweatshirt in the dryer for just a couple of minutes and put it on as soon as I can to keep the warmth next to my body. Oh, how cozy I feel. We also see the south wind brings a quietness to the earth.

"When he quieteth the earth." This word *quiet* means to be tranquil, to be at peace, to be undisturbed. How many people today are looking for just a little peace and quiet? Over the years, prescription drugs have been on the rise. We have seen an influx of drugs that offer tranquility. I am not saying that I am against someone taking medicine; however, I have found a peace that can outlast any drug on the market. It's the south wind of undisturbed peace that will quiet and warm my very soul.

Job has something else to tell us about the south wind, which is a golden nugget for sure: "Out of the *south* cometh the whirlwind" (Job 37:9; emphasis added). When I decided to look up the word *south*, I could hardly contain myself.

The words for south are *inner chamber*, a *private place*, a *parlor*. In the Bible, the inner chamber was the bedroom, so what I learned is that to have the south wind warm and quiet me, I must be in the inner chamber of his presence.

There is another wonderful story in the New Testament of a time when the south wind blew. There was a ship headed to Italy, and Paul had tried to warn those aboard that the weather was not conducive for travel, but the owner of the ship said to set sail, so away they went: "And when the south wind blew softly, supposing that they had obtained [their] purpose, loosing [thence], they sailed close by Crete" (Acts 27:13). Did you notice the description of the south wind? It blew softly. The New International Version says the south wind blew gently.

The north wind is a wind of cleansing; the south wind is a wind of renewal—soft, gentle, and tranquil. There's just one problem for many of us. When everything is good, peaceful, and calm, we sometimes think we have arrived. This is exactly what the scripture says: in the King James, they supposed that they had obtained their purpose, the Amplified Bible says they thought they had gained their objective, and the New International Version says they thought that they had obtained what they wanted.

How many times have we gotten what we wanted only to find out that God had something better for us. Not only did they think they arrived, but the real concern is that the Bible says they sailed close to Crete. The word *Crete* means fleshy or carnality. I do not want to feed my flesh or my carnal nature by being satisfied just because all is well.

Oh No, Not the Euroclydon

After the south wind blew so sweetly in the next verse, they hit a storm. "But not long after there arose against it a tempestuous wind called the Euroclydon" (Acts 27:14). Look at this in the NIV: "Before very long, a wind of hurricane force, called the "northeaster," swept down from the island." Let's not forget about the Amplified Version: "But soon afterward a violent wind [of the character of a typhoon], called a northeaster, came bursting down from the island."

We have a tempestuous wind, which means a violent storm, something turbulent or uncontrolled. Then this storm is defined by the word *hurricane*, a fast forceful tropical storm with torrential rains and winds. Then this Euroclydon is described as a violent wind or a typhoon. This is quite a storm after such a sweet soft south wind. The word *Euroclydon* simply means a northeaster.

The north wind cleanses; the south winds renews. But what happens when the north wind meets the wind from the east?

The East Wind

The east wind has several definitions. The first I want to look at is found in Genesis. The story is the dream of the Pharaoh where corn stalks appear, and the Bible says in

Genesis 41:23, "And, behold, seven ears, withered, thin and blasted with the east wind sprung up after them." Did you notice they were blasted by this wind? Other definitions of the word *blasted*: express annoyance, irritating, and flaming, or to scorch.

The next time we meet the east wind, God uses it to bring in the locusts: "And Moses stretched forth his rod over the land of Egypt and the LORD brought an east wind upon the land all that day and all that night and when it was morning the east wind brought the locusts" (Exodus 10:13). "The east wind carrieth him away and he departeth and as a storm hurleth him out of his place; the east wind is compared to a storm" (Job 27:21).

In the book of Isaiah, we have more detail on the east wind: "In measure it shooteth forth, thou wilt debate with it: he stayeth his rough wind in the day of the east wind" (Isaiah 27:8). Oh no, not only does the east windblast bring a storm, but now we see that this wind is rough. A definition of the word *rough* means severe or unpleasant.

One last scripture and I will fill you in on the purpose for the east wind: "And it came to pass, when the sun did arise that God prepared a vehement east wind and the sun beat upon the head of Jonah that he fainted and wished in himself to die. And said 'It is better for me to die than to live'" (Jonah 4:8). Now we see this wind as a vehement wind. From The Message Bible, it is called a hot blistering wind; and in the New International Version, it is once again a scorching wind; and finally from The Amplified Bible, it is a sultry east wind. Sultry means oppressively hot and damp, sticky or muggy.

Well, it's time to reveal the mission of the east wind—it is a wind of correction. God used this wind to get Jonah's attention. He also corrected Egypt when he brought in the locusts. Not too many people like to be corrected, but we all need the east wind to keep us on course.

I remember reading the book of Hebrews, and in chapter 11, I loved all the great heroes of faith, but then I would dread the next chapter on discipline and correction. I know we all need to be chastised by the hand of God, but always remember He is not a child abuser; He always disciplines us as his children—in love.

Then one day during my Bible time, I sensed that God wanted to tell me something, and I was headed to the chastisement chapter when I heard the voice of the lord in my inner man say to me, "Chastisement is correction for new directions." That was all I needed to hear: let the east wind blow and please, God, keep all of us on course to do your will.

The West Wind

I think the wind most spoken of is the south and then the north and east. And now we will look at the wind from the west. "And the LORD turned a mighty strong *west wind* which took away the locust and cast them into the Red sea;

there remained not one locust in all the coasts of Egypt" (Exodus 10:19; emphasis added). The Amplified Bible says a violent west wind lifted the locust and drove them from Egypt.

Let's dissect this verse. First, it says the Lord turned a mighty (a force of abundance), strong (firm, hard, severe) west wind. The word *west* means to roar. We see God turn the strong force of his abundance when he roared from the west, and the locust were driven out of the land. The west wind reverses the curse and brings in the blessings of God.

Now that we have the teaching on the four winds, we can turn to a very familiar story in the Old Testament and have it come alive to each of us. It is the story of the vision of the valley of dry bones found in Ezekiel chapter 37. How many wonderful sermons have been preached from this text, I wonder. Most preachers love verse 7: "So I prophesied as I was commanded and as I prophesied there was a noise and behold a shaking and the bones came together, bone to his bone."

There came a noise, then a shaking, and then the bones began to come together. Wow, and eventually they stood up to be a great army. What a vision, what excitement! Nevertheless, in the midst of all these great happenings, the Bible said they had no life in them. Hmm, we can have a noise, we can have a shaking and still no life?

The verses that I think are the greatest in this story are Ezekiel 37:9–10:

> Then said he unto me, "Prophesy unto the wind, prophesy, son of man and say to the wind, Thus saith the Lord GOD; *Come from the four winds* O breath and breathe upon these slain that they may live." So I prophesied as he commanded me, the breath came into them and they lived and stood up upon their feet, an exceeding great army. (emphasis added)

Whenever we get in a dry place or a dry season in our life and walk with the Lord, don't forget to call forth the four winds: "Come north wind and cleanse me, come south wind and renew me, come east wind and correct me, and come west wind and bless me. Oh, breathe on us Spirit of the Living God."

3

VESSELS OF HONOR

How many times have we asked the Lord, "What is your will for my life?" Every time I have an open forum or a prayer line, someone will undoubtedly ask this question.

Scripture makes it very clear what God's will is: "For this is the will of God, even your sanctification that ye should abstain from fornication that every one of you should know how to possess his vessel in sanctification and honor" (1 Thessalonians 4:3–4). From this verse, we see that God calls our bodies a vessel. As you know, we are a spirit, we have a soul, and we live in a body (1 Thess. 5:23). There are many different types of vessels in the Bible, just as there are many different body types. I am sure you have seen the pictures that describe us as a pear or apple-shaped. As we allow the Spirit of God to mold us and shape us into the vessel He desires us to be, our part is to honor Him.

"But now, O LORD, thou art our father; we are the clay, and thou our potter; and we all are the work of thy hand"

(Isaiah 64:8). Before a vessel can be of use, it must be shaped by the potter's hand. I love this verse that tells us that we are the work of his hand. Clay has to be prepared and shaped and fired before it has strength and durability.

One of my favorite verses is about us being a vessel for God: "But we have this treasure in earthen vessels, that the excellency of the power may be of God, and not of us" (2 Corinthians 4:7). We must at all times remember that we are just earthen vessels, and once the clay has been shaped into the form the potter desires, he then puts his creation into a fire.

Many years ago, I took a class on pottery; I wanted to start with the easiest thing I could make. So I decided to do a Christmas tree. There were only two pieces of clay that came from a mold, and when the pieces were put together, the tree had a large seam running down the middle of the piece. At this stage, the clay had not been fired so it was greenware my instructor told me to be very careful as it was a fragile object. I tried to remove the seam with a small piece of steel wool. I was supposed to rub the seam softly as to remove the line and then we could put the tree into the kiln.

I destroyed the first tree because I was too heavy-handed and my finger went right through the top of the tree, so I had to purchase another tree, and I was ever so careful with this one little tiny circles with no pressure, and I was finally able to finish this and put the tree into the kiln. Once it was fired, it was strong, and I didn't have to worry about touching it or breaking it.

Many times, God puts us into the fire. In the Bible, it says that even our faith is tested by fire. So let me share three things I have learned about the testing of the Lord by fire: First, every test is timed. God knows how much we can handle, and just as in school we were given a time limit for each test, so God knows the beginning from the end. The second thing I learned is that during the time of testing, you don't receive any answers while the test is in progress. Once the time of the test is over and the papers are handed in, so to speak, you can ask the teacher or professor for any answer, and it will be freely given to you. How many times in my life during a season of testing or fire I have had a hard time hearing the Lord. But once the test is over and I look back, I can see His hand clearly and know the purpose for this test. The third and final thing I had to learn is that if you fail the test, you get to take it over and over and over again. How I love the Lord's patience with us that He wants us to succeed and be promoted. But He needs to ensure that we have learned what ever the valuable lesson He was trying to teach us.

I used my Christmas tree for many, many years and because it was fired and glazed, it was something of beauty that I displayed every December. We too are vessels that have been through the fires of life, shaped by the potter's hand to display his glory and to shine for Him and His kingdom as vessels of honor.

A Vessel of Honor

Timothy will give us some insight as to a vessel of honor: "But in a great house there are not only vessels of gold and of silver but also of wood and of earth and some to honor and some to dishonour" (2 Timothy 2:20). Before I can share on the vessel of honor, we need to understand the term *dishonor* from the above passage.

When we hear the word *dishonor*, we think of something shameful or something that has brought disgrace—he got a dishonorable discharge from the military or they brought dishonor on the family name—so this word must be explained in view of the Bible language and times.

To us in the western world, the word *dishonor* means loss of respect, shame or failure, to treat disrespectfully, to discredit. However, in these verses in Timothy, the it has an entirely different meaning—it means of less esteem. On the other hand, another way to say it is less value, but not without any value.

We can see this clearly from our scripture about articles found in a house. First, we will see the honorable vessels, gold and silver. Gold is very costly, as well as silver, but gold is more costly. That does not mean silver is worthless; it just means it is worth less than gold. Both have intricate value, and if you prefer gold, you will spend more to acquire gold than if you purchase silver.

I have an easy way to explain this: I had a friend named Donna who loved Hummels (the little figurines from Germany), and her husband would buy her one for each special occasions—her birthday, Christmas, or Mother's Day. Donna always had them on display; she had her husband build her a curio cabinet, and these little figurines would sit on a doily and look lovely under the lights. She acquired a very attractive display.

Blue Light Special

One day I was in Kmart, and all of a sudden, I saw a blue light flashing, women running, and the announcer yelling, "Blue-light special figurines on sale today, this hour only." Well, being the wise women that I am and not wanting to miss a special, I ran with the rest of the pack.

There on a table were little figurines, some even similar to the Hummel's that Donna collected. I bought one with a little boy and girl on a school bench. It reminded me of my daughter and son. I went home with a smile on my face, change in my pocket, and a cute figurine.

Now my figurine was not put in a cabinet on lace under hot lights (for fear the plastic would melt); I put it in a shelf in my family room. In addition, when I went to remove the price tag, there it was—Made in Taiwan. What, not Germany?

I had a vessel, and as long as I didn't put my copy next to an original, I would be fine. But could you picture me taking my Taiwan blue-light special over to Donna's house and asking to put it in display next to hers? It would be obvious that mine was a cheap imitation.

Here is a little lesson on the two words we are talking about, honor and dishonor. Both items had value, and both items had worth; however, one was more costly than the other.

Fresh Water Daily

A vessel of honor was simply a vessel carried by women who would fill this container daily with fresh water to meet all the needs of her family. In the Old Testament, it was a requirement for the men of God to wash their hands and feet as they entered the sanctuary to worship God. In the foyer or vestibule, there would be a large wooden vessel filled with clean water for their cleansing and a large wooden bowl for them to put the water into after they cleansed themselves—one a vessel of honor and one of dishonor or lesser value.

I saw this for myself when I went to Israel in 2000. Before the Jewish men approached the Wailing wall, there was a large white concrete basin, and attached to this were golden pots on silver chains. I really wasn't sure what I was seeing until a man approached this basin. He then poured water into the golden pot, washed and dumped the used water into the basin around the container. Here I was in Israel seeing in person a vessel of honor and a vessel of dishonor. The vessel with the water was the vessel of honor, and the container used to receive the water that had been used was the vessel of dishonor or lesser. Remember: both were needed, and both had value. What a thrill to have the scriptures come alive before my very eyes!

The Choice is Yours

The word of God gives us a choice as to what vessel we desire to be. We can all be a vessel of honor prepared for God's uses—but on one condition.

Let us see the conditions of our choice: "But in a great house there are not only vessels of gold and of silver but also of wood and of earth and some to honor and some to dishonour. If a man, therefore purge himself from these he shall be a vessel unto honour, sanctified and meet for the master's use, and prepared unto every good work" (2 Tim. 2:20–21). What do we need to be purged from? "Nevertheless the foundation of God standeth sure, having this seal, The Lord knoweth them that are his. And, let everyone that nameth the name of Christ depart from iniquity" (2 Tim. 2:19).

In order to be a vessel of honor, we must depart from *iniquity*. Let's define this old English word so we can better understand the part we play as we are being prepared for every good work.

Iniquity: anything injustice or immoral. The thesaurus helps us better understand this word as sin, evil, vice. May the Lord help each of us depart from sin and evil. What about the word *purge*? Sounds painful to me; however, its definition is quite freeing: to remove something undesirable, to free somebody from guilt or sin.

When we repent, God cleanses us and fills us with His living waters, and we become a vessel of honor for Him. Each day, we should ask for a fresh infilling of His Spirit. Even in scripture, Jesus said His spirit was rivers of living water. How refreshing it is to be cleansed and purged and prepared for His service.

There is a man who is very familiar to us in the New Testament; his name is Saul, and when he encountered the Lord his name was changed to Paul. He is not only a vessel of honor, but God called him a chosen vessel.

A Chosen Vessel

Saul was a devoted Old Testament Jew, and his own testimony is found in Acts 22:3: "I am verily a man which am a Jew, born in Tarsus, a city in Cilicia yet brought up in this city at the feet of Gamaliel and taught according to the perfect manner of the law of the fathers and was zealous toward God."

Who is this man named Gamaliel? Acts 5:34 gives us insight as to Saul's teacher: "Then stood there up one in the council a Pharisee named Gamaliel a doctor of the law, held in reputation among all the people." The Amplified Bible said he (Gamaliel) was highly esteemed as a teacher of the law. Therefore, it was well established that Saul knew one of the greatest teachers of his day and was taught the word of God.

Just as a sidenote, the name *Gamaliel* means "benefits of the Lord." And how true it is whenever we study or are taught the word of God we receive great spiritual benefits.

Before his conversion, Saul persecuted the church, thinking that these believers were leaving their Jewish beliefs. The first time we meet him is in the book of Acts, and his opening was anything but flattering. In Acts 7, there was a young man named Stephen, who was a deacon, and the religious leaders were about to kill him; they would cast stones or bludgeon him to death.

A Mad Man Among Us

Saul guarded the clothes of the men who were stoning Stephen to death. They cast him out of the city and stoned him, and the witnesses laid down their clothes at a young man's feet whose name was Saul (Acts 7:58). This story gets worse from this point on: after Stephen dies, in Acts 8, we see Saul consenting to his death, and after Stephen is buried, Saul makes havoc on the believers.

As for Saul, he made havoc of the church, entering into every house and haling men and women and committed them to prison (Acts 8:3). The Amplified Bible says he shamefully treated them with cruelty and violence. His own testimony years later is in Acts 26:11: "And I punished them oft in every synagogue and compelled them to blaspheme and being exceedingly mad against them I persecuted them even unto strange cites." Other versions render it as to have an obsession against, to be in bitter fury, to act as a maniac, to be enraged and furious.

Do you get a picture of this man? He is out of control and enraged in anger. One last witness is in Acts 22:19, where he tells us that not only did he imprison the saints, but he also beat them in the synagogues. Can you image being in church and a man comes up the aisle and begins to punch and beat the men in the congregation? Outrageous behavior, isn't it?

I See the Light, I See the Light

Saul was on his way to Damascus with approval to continue to abuse the saints, and during his travel, he had an encounter of the strangest kind:

> And Saul, yet breathing out threatenings and slaughter against the disciples of the Lord, went unto the high priest and desired of him letters to Damascus to the synagogues, that if he found any of this way, whether they were men or women, he might bring them bound unto Jerusalem. And as he journeyed, he came near Damascus and suddenly there shined round about him a light from heaven.

> And he fell to the earth and heard a voice saying unto him "Saul, Saul, why persecutest thou me?" And he said "Who art thou, Lord?" And the Lord said "I am Jesus whom thou persecutest." (Acts 9:1–5)

When Saul got up, he was blind due to the bright light, and they had to lead him into Damascus. He was there for three days fasting and praying. The Lord gave him a vision that a disciple named Ananias would come and pray for him, and he would receive his sight. At first, Ananias didn't want to go. Could you blame him? I would not want to go either. Nevertheless, the Lord spoke to him, and he obeyed and went to minister to Saul.

What the Lord said to Ananias concerning Saul is quite amazing considering Paul's behavior. He said: "Go thy way for he is a chosen vessel unto me, to bear my name before the Gentiles and kings and the children of Israel" (Acts 9:15). "A chosen vessel," and God said that the chosen vessel would bear his name.

One day, each of us will have a new name. Look at these wonderful promises:

> And the Gentiles shall see thy righteousness and all kings thy glory and thou shalt be called by a new name which the mouth of the LORD shall name. (Isa. 62:2)

> And him that overcometh will I make a pillar in the temple of my God and he shall go no more out and

> I will write upon him the name of my God and the name of the city of my God which is new Jerusalem, which cometh down out of heaven from my God and I will write upon him my new name. (Rev. 3:12)

Something else is very important about these verses. All of us have seen fine china, and some are blessed enough to own a set. One thing is noticeable on a chosen vessel if you turn it over—there will be a name inscribed, most times, in gold. When I received my first piece of Lenox, it was Christmas gift from my daughter. She had gotten me a lovely candy dish. When I turned it over, it did not say candy dish on the bottom. Why not? Because the important thing is the creator, not the container!

I have never seen a plate with the name on the bottom that says plate, or a coffee cup that says cup. Nevertheless, I had seen engraving such as Waterford, Noritake, Royal Dolton. Thanks be to God, no matter what our past, he has chosen us and wants to anoint us to be a vessel for him.

I trust you look forward to the day when our God and creator writes his name on us. Oh, happy day! I want to end this chapter with a poem called the "Chosen Vessel." I don't know the author, but what a blessing this poem has been to me.

The Chosen Vessel

The Master was searching for a vessel to use;
Before him were many,
Which one would he choose?

"Take me" cried the gold one,
"I'm shiny and bright,
I am of great value and I do things just right.
My beauty and luster will outshine the rest
And for someone like you, master,
Gold would be best."

The Master passed on with no word at all
And looked at a silver urn narrow and tall.
"I'll serve you, dear Master; I'll pour out your wine,
I will be on your table whenever you dine.
My lines are so graceful,
My carvings so true
And silver will always compliment you."

Unheeding the Master passed on to the brass,
Wide-mouthed, shallow and polished like glass.
"Here! Here!" Cried the vessel, "I know I will do
Place me on your table for all men to view."
"Look at me "called the goblet of crystal so clear
"My transparency shows my contents so dear.
"Through fragile am I, I will serve you with pride
And I'm sure I'll be happy in your house to abide."

The Master came next to a vessel of wood,
Polished and carved it solidly stood.
"You may use me, dear Master,"
The wooden bowl said
But I'd rather you use me for fruit, not for bread."
Then the Master looked down and saw a vessel of clay,
Empty and broken it helplessly lay.
No hope had the vessel
That the Master might choose
To cleanse and make whole, to fill and to use.

"Ah! I have been hoping this vessel to find.
I will mend it, use it and make it all mine.
I need not the vessel with pride of itself
Nor one that is narrow to sit on the shelf
Nor one that is big-mouthed, shallow and loud
Nor one that displays his contents so proud.
Not the one that thinks he can do all things just right
But this plain, earthly vessel filled with power and
might."

Then gently he lifted the vessel of clay
Mended and cleansed it and filled it that day.
Spoke to it kindly–"There's work you must do -
Just pour out to others, as I pour into you."

4

THE SEVEN SPRINKLINGS

In biblical times, people and objects were sprinkled, sometimes with water, oil, or blood. A very interesting verse in the book of 1 Peter 1:2 is "Elect according to the foreknowledge of God the Father, through Sanctification of the Spirit unto obedience and sprinkling of the Blood of Jesus." ("To God's elect, who have been chosen according to the foreknowledge of God the Father through the sanctifying work of the Spirit to be obedient to Jesus Christ and sprinkled with his blood" [NIV].)

This one verse is a preacher's dream: first there is the elect. I wonder how many sermons I have heard on being the elect of God? Then we have God's foreknowledge. And how about the wonderful subject of sanctification? Many years ago, this verse caught my attention with the phrase "the sprinkling of the blood." I wondered what the scriptures had to say about the blood being sprinkled. This led to a wonderful truth that I cannot wait to share.

Moses was the first to sprinkle blood: the Bible says that Moses, on the night of the first Passover, was to kill a lamb and dip hyssop in the blood and to apply it to the doorposts of their homes. The story is found in the book of Exodus. The children of God had been enslaved in Egypt for over four hundred years, God had sent nine plagues, and the tenth plague was the death of every firstborn child. Every Hebrew home was to have the blood of an innocent lamb sprinkled on their doors, and God said that when He saw the blood, he would pass over them, thus, the name *Passover*.

I find it interesting that when the story is being told of Moses leaving the house of Pharaoh and becoming the great deliverer, in the New Testament book of Hebrews, the writer uses this description of the Passover: "Through faith, he kept the Passover and the sprinkling of blood lest he that destroyed the firstborn should touch them" (Heb. 11:28).

It is important you understand that this sprinkled blood of the Passover was really Jesus's blood as we are told in 1 Corinthians 5:7b: "For even Christ our *Passover* is sacrificed for us" (emphasis added). Why was He sacrificed for us? John the Baptists makes this so clear in John 1:29: "The next day John seeth Jesus coming unto him, and saith, Behold the Lamb of God, which takes away the sin of the world. He became our Passover lamb so that our sins could be forgiven."

We have been redeemed thru his sprinkled blood. "Forasmuch as ye know that ye were not redeemed with corruptible things, as silver and gold, from your vain conversation received by tradition from your fathers But with the precious blood of Christ, as of a *lamb* without blemish and without spot" (1 Peter 1:18–19; emphasis added).

The book of Revelation tells us about the song of Moses: "And they sing the song of Moses the servant of God, and the song of the Lamb, saying, Great and marvelous are thy works, Lord God Almighty; just and true are thy ways, thou King of saints" (Rev. 15:3).

Cleansing of the Leper

Now we will look at a time when a person, not a doorframe, would be sprinkled with blood. Leviticus 14:1–7 is a law and ritual for cleansing from leprosy.

> And the LORD spake unto Moses, saying, "This shall be the law of the leper in the day of his cleansing: He shall be brought unto the priest and the priest shall go forth out of the camp and the priest shall look and behold, if the plague of leprosy be healed in the leper. Then shall the priest command to take for him that is to be cleansed two birds alive and clean, and cedar wood and scarlet and hyssop. And the priest shall command that one of the birds be killed in an earthen vessel over running water. And as for the living bird, he shall take it and the cedar wood and the scarlet and the hyssop, and shall dip them and the living bird in the blood of the bird

> that was killed over the running water and he shall
> sprinkle upon him that is to be cleansed from the
> leprosy seven times and shall pronounce him clean,
> and shall let the living bird loose into the open
> field."

There are so many things to look at in this portion of scripture; however, I want you to notice that this was done for a leper who was cleansed. Several important things are mentioned. Look at verse 4, we have cedar wood, scarlet, and hyssop; and in the next verse, there is water and an earthen vessel. Finally, after the death of the innocent sacrifice, blood was sprinkled on the person seven times, and they were pronounced clean.

Let me explain how this ceremony was conducted. One bird was laid on a piece of cedar wood, and then a branch from the hyssop tree was put on the bird's chest, a scarlet thread then secured it.

Many times in the Bible, there are shadows and types, hidden stories within a story. Have you ever seen the children's magazine called *Highlights*? They have a picture, and hidden within the photos are other objects that are not so clear and visible; children are encouraged to find the hidden objects. It is like that with this story in Leviticus. Let us look with the eye of faith and see this story within a story.

Cedar Wood, Hyssop, and Scarlet

The cedar tree is very tall (2 Kings 19:23). The Lord said he dwells in a house of cedar (2 Sam. 7:2). The temple of Solomon was furnished with cedar wood (1 Kings 19:11). The cedar was in the garden of God (Ezek. 31:8), and people have at times called the cedar tree the king of all trees. Is it a possibility that our King was nailed to a cedar cross?

Just as the cedar is the tallest of trees, the hyssop is very small in comparison; the hyssop has branches shaped like a paintbrush. The first time it appears for us is in Exodus 12 on the night of the first Passover. God told Moses to kill a lamb and to dip the hyssop in blood, so the first time it was used, it involved the death of an innocent lamb. When is the last time we see *hyssop* in the word of God? Would you believe that it also is in conjunction with a lamb? This time, however, it is God's Son whom John called the lamb of God.

Our reference is in John 19:28–30:

> After this, Jesus knowing, that all things were now accomplished that the Scripture might be fulfilled, saith "I Thirst." Now there was set a vessel full of vinegar and they filled a sponge with vinegar and put it upon hyssop and put it to his mouth. When Jesus therefore had received the vinegar, he said "It is finished." and he bowed his head and gave up the ghost.

Hyssop represents cleansing from sin. David said in Psalm 51:7, "Purge me with hyssop and I shall be clean; wash me, and I shall be whiter than snow."

The sacrifice was placed on the cedar tree by a scarlet cord. Let us take a quick look at the scarlet thread in Genesis 38:27–28: "And it came to pass in the time of her travail, that, behold, twins were in her womb and it came to pass when she travailed that the one put out his hand and the midwife took and bound upon his hand a scarlet thread saying, 'This came out first.'" So the first time we see a scarlet thread is in the book of Genesis to clearly mark the firstborn. How thankful I am that Jesus is the firstborn among many brothers!

I think the most familiar story we can relate to about a scarlet thread is when the walls of Jericho were about to fall to the ground. Joshua had promised a woman named Rahab that if she would hang a scarlet thread out of her window, she and her entire family would be saved (Joshua 2:18).

Only Jesus, God's firstborn son, can save us. And even when he was about to die, they draped him in a scarlet robe. And they stripped him and put on him a scarlet robe. Moreover, when they had platted a crown of thorns, put it upon his head, and a reed in his right hand, they bowed the knee before him and mocked him, saying, "Hail, King of the Jews!" (Matt. 27:27–28).

Jesus died on a tree so that his blood would cleanse us and through the scarlet thread our families can also be saved by faith in his atonement, and he will sprinkle us with his precious blood and cleanse from all sin, just like the leper who was cleansed and sprinkled with blood and water seven times.

The First of Seven

We will now look at how his blood was sprinkled seven times. The first account is in the Gospel of Luke: Jesus was eight days old, and his parents brought him to the temple to dedicate him to God and to have him circumcised (Luke 2:21). This was the first time that he shed his blood on earth.

Today we have our male children circumcised for reasons of hygiene; however, circumcision has more than just a natural reason—it has a spiritual meaning. Even the word *circumcision* itself reveals much; it means to cut. This cutting and shedding of blood was a seal of righteousness—now you belong to God. Look at what the book of Acts reveals to us: "And he gave him the covenant of circumcision and so Abraham begat Isaac and circumcised him the eighth day" (Acts 7:8). In addition, in Romans 4:11, it speaks of Abraham: "And he received the sign of circumcision, a seal of the righteousness that he had by faith while he was still uncircumcised."

The first sprinkling of the blood of Jesus is to bring us back to God and to circumcise our hearts by his spirit.

"For he is not a Jew, which is one outwardly neither is that circumcision which is outward in the flesh but he is a Jew, which is one inwardly; and circumcision is that of the heart, in the spirit and not in the letter; whose praise is not of men but of God" (Rom. 2:27–29).

Jesus sprinkled his blood as an infant to bring God's blood back into the earth. The first Adam had the blood of God. When he sinned, the bloodline was not pure anymore, so Jesus came as the Last Adam (1 Cor. 15:45) to get God's blood on the earth so that we could enter into blood covenant with God whether Gentile or natural Jew.

The book of Acts puts it so beautifully in Acts 20:28: "Take heed therefore unto yourselves and to all the flock over the which the Holy Ghost hath made you overseers, to feed the church of God which he hath purchased with his own blood." The shedding of his blood at circumcision was to enable a blood covenant with God and men who would receive it.

The Second Sprinkling

Jesus sprinkled his blood in the garden of Gethsemane found in the gospel of Luke: "And being in an agony he prayed more earnestly: and his sweat was as it were great drops of blood falling down to the ground" (Lk 22:44). Here we see him bleeding due to agony and pressure.

We have all had a garden of Gethsemane in our lives; we pray "not my will but thy will be done." Jesus prayed this three times to the point of bleeding. Whenever we find ourselves being pressed (Gethsemane means the pressing of an olive), we do not need to shed our blood for obedience, but we may need to call on the blood of Jesus. When we have a hard time obeying the Lord and struggling with our wills yet in our hearts we want God's will, apply the blood of Jesus for obedience. Remember, we have a blood covenant, and we can obey God no matter what agony we face.

The Third Sprinkling

Jesus was always obedient to the will of God, and in John 19:1, we see him bleeding for the third time. Then Pilate therefore took Jesus and scourged him. Another word for scourged from the New International is *flogged* or *whipped*. The prophet Isaiah foretold this in Isaiah 53:4–5: "Surely, he hath borne our grief's and carried our sorrows, yet we did esteem him stricken, smitten of God and afflicted. But, he was wounded for our transgressions, he was bruised for our iniquities; the chastisement of our peace was upon him and with his stripes we are healed."

Jesus was scourged so that this sprinkling of blood could be for the physical healing of our bodies. With his stripes, we are healed.

In the Old Testament, God promised to be our healer. One of the most famous verses is found in Exodus 15:26. "If thou wilt diligently hearken to the voice of the Lord thy

God and wilt do that which is right in His sight and wilt give ear to his commandments and keep all his statutes, I will put none of the diseases upon thee which I have brought upon the Egyptians for I am the Lord that healeth thee." In this verse, God names himself Jehovah Rapha. (*Rapha* is the word for physician or doctor.)

In the New Testament, there are several scriptures that make it known that it is God's will to heal us and that Jesus did not suffer the stripes in vain. In Acts 10:38, it says, "Now God anointed Jesus of Nazareth with the Holy Ghost and power, who went about doing good and healing all that were oppressed of the devil for God was with him." There is a promise in 1 Peter 2:24, which brings us back again to Isaiah that by his stripes or by the sprinkled blood we are healed: "Who his own self bare our sins in his own body on the tree, that we being dead to sins, should live unto righteousness by whose stripes ye were healed." When you are in need of healing, sprinkle the blood of Jesus and pray for healing.

The Fourth Sprinkling

The fourth time Jesus shed his blood is in John 19:2: "And the soldiers plaited a crown of thorns and put it on his head and they put on him a purple robe and said 'Hail, King of the Jews!' and they smote him with their hands." Unless you have been to Israel, you cannot envision the crown of thorns. I was able to go to Israel in the year 2000, and I was really taken aback when I saw the size of the thorns on their bushes. We think of a tiny prick when we handle a rose bush or something with a thorn; however, the ones in Israel are quite large and thick. These soldiers wanted to torture Jesus, so I am sure there were many thorns tightly woven together in this mock crown.

Why the crown of thorns? There are a couple of reasons for this fourth sprinkling. In the Garden of Eden, once sin entered into the heart of man, he was no longer at leisure in the garden.

> And unto Adam he said "because thou hast hearkened unto the voice of thy wife and hast eaten of the tree of which I commanded thee, saying 'Thou shall not eat of it' cursed is the ground for thy sake; in sorrow shalt thou eat of it all the days of thy life. Thorns also and thistles shall it bring forth to thee and thou shalt eat the herb of the field; in the sweat of thy face shalt thou eat bread till thou return unto the ground for out of it wast thou taken." (Genesis 3:17–19)

The first time we see thorns is when the ground was cursed, and now Adam will till in the sweat of his brow. Can you make the connection that the thorns were on the brow of Jesus to redeem us even from the curse on the earth?

However, I believe there is another reason that thorns were placed around the head of Jesus: it was to overcome the evil that can attack our minds. In the Old Testament, Belial is another name for Satan (2 Cor. 6:15), and we are told that evil and wicked people were called the sons of Belial, and reference is made that these sons of Belial (demons) are thorns. We can read in Joshua 23:13: "Know for a certainty that the Lord your God will no more drive out any of the nations from before you but they shall be snares and traps unto you; scourges in your sides and thorns in you eyes." And in 1 Samuel 23:6, "But the sons of Belial shall be all of them as thorns thrust away."

Lastly, I believe the crown of thorns can help us conquer the fiery darts of the devil, which are words or thoughts that are not from God. I believe the crown of thorns was so that we can acquire peace of mind. "And let the peace of God which passeth all understanding, keep your hearts and minds though Christ Jesus" (Phil. 4:7).

Remember in Isaiah 53:5, "The chastisement of our peace was upon Him."

The Fifth Sprinkling

The fifth sprinkling of the blood of Jesus happened on the cross: "They pierced my hands and feet" (Psalm 22:16b). How can we apply this to our lives? This should be used in conjunction with our works (hands) and our walk (feet). Do not forget to apply his blood to your everyday life and activities.

The Sixth Sprinkling

After Jesus had died on the cross, there was yet another shedding of His blood: "But one of the soldiers with a spear pierced his side and forthwith came blood and water" (John 19:34). This blood was for our victory and the water for the cleansing that we need on and daily basis: "Who is he that overcometh the world but he that believeth that Jesus is the son of God, this is he that came by water and blood, even Jesus Christ; not by water only but by water and blood" (1 John 5:5–6). The book of Ephesians says the water of the word washes us. Thank God for the water and the blood.

Where is the Seventh Sprinkling?

On the Day of Atonement in Leviticus chapter 16, the high priest would sprinkle blood on the mercy seat seven times. Please remember that the mercy seat in the wilderness tabernacle was only a shadow of the real thing. Something wonderful happened after Jesus died; he ascended into heaven, and I believe it was his blood sprinkled for the seventh time on the mercy seat. How did I come to this conclusion?

On Sunday, we find Mary in the garden wanting to anoint Jesus's body, and she does not find him in the tomb. As he approaches her, she thinks that he is an attendant at the graveside and asks what happened to Jesus body. The moment he speaks her name, she knows it's Jesus, and she falls at this feet. He then tells her not to touch him or hold on to him, that he must first ascend to his father and her God (Jn. 20:17).

Jesus appeared to his disciples, and Thomas was not there. He could not believe the disciples had seen a risen Jesus and even went so far as to say, "When I can put my hand in the wound in His side then I will believe" (Jn. 20:27). So we see Mary who was a devoted follower being told not to touch him, and yet in the next few verses, He appears and tells Thomas to reach out and touch him (Jn. 20:27). Why was doubting Thomas encouraged to touch and Mary the believer told not to touch him?

The book of Hebrews answers that question.

> Christ being come an high priest of good things to come, by a greater and more perfect tabernacle not made with hands, that is to say, not of this building. Neither by the blood of goats and calves but by his own blood, he entered in once into the holy place, having obtained eternal redemption for us. For if the blood of bulls and of goats and the ashes of an heifer sprinkling the unclean, sanctifieth to the purifying of the flesh how much more shall the blood of Christ, who through the eternal Spirit offered himself without spot to God, purge your conscience from dead works to serve the living God? (Heb. 9:11–14)

Jesus as our High Priest entered once into heaven, and His blood became the sacrifice that far outweighed the offerings of bulls and goats. The number seven is a number of completion and finality.

Did you know that the blood of Jesus speaks from heaven? "To the church of the firstborn, whose names are written in heaven, you have come to God the Judge of all, to the spirits of the righteous made perfect, to Jesus the mediator of a new covenant and to the sprinkled blood that speaks a better word than the blood of Abel" (Hebrews 12:23–24, NIV). We do not get the full effect of his blood speaking until we understand about Abel.

In Genesis, Cain kills his brother, Abel, and something very powerful is revealed: "The LORD said to Cain: 'Where is Abel thy brother?' and he said 'I know not! Am I my brother's keeper?' and he said 'What hast thou done; the voice of thy brother's blood crieth unto me from the ground'" (Gen. 4:9–10). God hears the blood of Abel crying from the ground. The Amplified Bible really clears this up in Hebrews 12:24: "And to Jesus, the Mediator [go-between or agent] of a new covenant and to the sprinkled blood, which speaks [of mercy] a better, nobler, and more gracious message than the blood of Abel [which cried out for vengeance]."

I know that if God heard Abel's blood from the ground, how much more He hears the blood of Jesus when he speaks from heaven. And please notice that Abel's blood wanted revenge; Jesus's blood speaks mercy.

The seventh sprinkling of the blood of Jesus is so that he can speak mercy over my life and yours.

I am so grateful for his sprinkled precious blood!

My prayer is that we all will walk in this teaching and be thankful for our blood covenant and be thankful for obedience in hard times, thankful for the healing of our bodies and for peace in our minds. We know everywhere we go and whatever we do his blood covers us. We remember the water of his word and the sprinkled blood on the cross washes us, and that God through Jesus Christ our Lord sheds mercy on us.

5

RX FOR HEALTH

There have been thousands of books written about healing. What do I hope to accomplish in just one chapter on such a controversial subject? My goal is to share just two important things that can help us to understand why sometimes we do not see our healing manifested, or we have prayed and not seen loved ones recover. I believe in divine healing as a work of redemption done on the cross of Calvary.

The prophecy in Isaiah 53:5 was "but he was wounded for our transgressions, he was bruised for our iniquities; the chastisement of our peace was upon him and with his stripes we are healed." This was fulfilled as a promise for us in Matthew 8:17 when the even was come, they brought unto him many that were possessed with devils and he cast out the spirits with his word and healed all that were sick "that it might be fulfilled which was spoken by Esaias the prophet, saying 'Himself took our infirmities, and bare our sicknesses.'"

Jesus healed all who were sick, and this is even *before* he was whipped and stripped on the cross for our healing. 1 Peter 2:24 makes this so clear for us: "Who his own self bare our sins in his own body on the tree, that we, being dead to sins should live unto righteousness: by whose stripes ye were healed." So the $64,000-dollar question is why aren't we healed?

The Benefits of the Lord

I want to start out with a very familiar psalm, it's Psalm 103:1–3: "Bless the LORD O my soul and all that is within me bless his holy name. Bless the LORD, O my soul and forget not all his benefits who forgiveth all thine iniquities, who healeth all thy diseases." Did you catch the phrase "don't forget your benefits"?

Let us do a scenario: you are applying for a job, and the first offer is a job at $15 an hour, however, there are no benefits. The second offer you have is for only $12 an hour to start, but it has a great benefit package. Which is the better offer? Well if you know anything about how expensive it is to get health insurance, for instance, you will take the second offer at less money because it is much more valuable than the first offer.

My husband was a union plumber for twenty-five years, and every three years they would revise the benefit plan for the family. I have to be honest and tell you that I never really read the new benefits; I just wanted to know if he got a raise.

Then when my daughter needed braces, I went to his benefit book to see our allowance and all the details that would follow. I did exactly what they required, and she had her braces. I had my reimbursement, and the dentist was paid in full, and what a beautiful smile my daughter has today.

Look at what His word tells us in Psalm 68:19: "Blessed be the Lord, who daily loadeth us with benefits, even the God of our salvation." I doubt that we are walking every day in all of the provision that He would like to load on us daily.

This brings me to another thought on Psalm 103 about forgetting his benefits. As I said, my husband had a good benefit plan, and his union would pay for any lab expense or x-rays when I would see my doctor. However, they did not cover the actual office visit, and every year I would pay for the physical visit.

On one occasion, we decided to go to a banquet the union was sponsoring. This affair was at a very nice country club, so I got all dressed up and even borrowed my mother's diamond earrings. After the usual introductions, the woman next to me started up a conversation. It went something like this: "Don't you just love the new benefit package?" And I thought, *Oh, what a long night this will be.* Surely, there are more interesting things to talk about than this. So to be polite, I asked her what were the new benefits she was so excited about? Only to hear that a couple of years ago, they included in the benefits that all doctor's office visits would be 100 percent covered. What?

For the last couple of years, I had paid my doctor and never once did the union contact me and ask if I would like to have my money refunded? The first thing I did when I got home was to grab that union benefit plan and read for myself that she had told me the truth. Why didn't I receive this provided benefit? Because I did not apply for what was already provided for me.

First thing Monday morning, I called my husband's union and asked how I could be reimbursed? They told me I needed to provide them with my cancelled check and a paid receipt from my doctor. They also insisted that I send these papers with a self-addressed envelope, and then they would issue a refund by check.

I complied completely, and I really had no doubt that the money was on the way. What am I trying to say? Many times, our healing and health is hindered because we do not understand our benefits and how they need to be applied for.

Why didn't I know the allotted allowance? Because I had not read the benefit book until I had a need. I fear many of us do not really know all the benefits of the Lord, and we do not read His word as we should until there is a need. Thank God he meets our needs, but we would be much better off if we knew ahead of time the benefits He has provided.

The Bible is our benefit book, and I do not just want to read it when I have a need, but to keep His word in my heart. And when a need arises, I will know what benefit He has already provided for me to apply for and to receive.

My question would be, do you know what your benefits are, and how do you receive them?

Did You Take Your Meds?

The second thing I want to share is our need to take the word of the Lord as medicine. It is written in Proverbs 4:20–22: "My son, attend to my words; incline thine ear unto my sayings. Let them not depart from thine eyes; keep them in the midst of thine heart for they are life unto those that find them and health to all their flesh." The Amplified Bible gives us a little more insight: "My son, attend to my words; consent and submit to my sayings. Let them not depart from your sight; keep them in the center of your heart for they are life to those who find them; healing and health to all their flesh."

We can see from this proverb that if we find the word of God and keep it, it will be health and healing to all our flesh. However, how does this happen? The word *health* when translated means to cure, to mend, to heal as a remedy of medicine. Let's look at some things we do to get the proper medicine.

For this illustration, I will use a small child who in the middle of the night wakes with a painful earache. As a parent or guardian, you know that this child will need a strong antibiotic. So there are several steps that must be taken to ensure healing for this child.

You Must Make an Appointment

First thing in the morning, you will call the pediatrician for an appointment. In all the years that I have made appointments to see a doctor, never once did the doctor or surgeon answer the phone when I called. You speak to a receptionist who will schedule an appointment for your child at their convenience. For this illustration, you are self-employed and the doctor's appointment is for 11:00 a.m., so there is a good chance you will miss a half-day of work and possibly lose some income.

You arrive at the doctor's office at 10:45 a.m. and sign in. You will be told to take a seat in the waiting room so you can wait to see the doctor. Remember you have an 11:00 a.m. appointment, and I trust you understand that you will not see the doctor at that hour. You wait, and you wait, and then when your name is called, they take you from the outer waiting room to the inner waiting room.

What is the difference between the two waiting rooms? The outer room has people, magazines, possibly a television, but the inner waiting room has none of these conveniences and then you are told something that can test your patience:

"The doctor will be right in." Finally, the doctor comes to examine the child and then he makes a diagnosis that the child has an ear infection. (Of course I already knew that!) The next step is to write a prescription for an antibiotic. You then dress the child and return to the outer office.

Something strange happens at this time even though the child is not one bit better after you pay the doctor. You then head to the closest pharmacy. At the pharmacy, you hand a piece of paper you cannot read to a man you do not know in a white jacket. (Please do not tell me you do not have faith.) In addition, this man will give you two options: wait or come back at a later time. Since the child is in pain, you wait again. Now you pay for the medicine and return home with the solution in hand.

Follow Directions

Every prescription comes with a label. First, it must be in your name, and there may be several warnings on the label that must be followed for the medicine to work at its full potential. If you are to take one teaspoon every four hours, and you decide that you want to recover at a faster rate, you take four teaspoons every hour. What will be the outcome? Some medicines need to be refrigerated, and if you disregard that warning and put the bottle on the stove while you roast a turkey, you will interfere with the ingredients of the prescription.

Once when my daughter had an ear infection, we were prescribed amoxicillin; this medicine was to be taken for ten days and stored in the refrigerator. After only a few doses, she began to feel better; however, I continued the full prescription even though the symptoms had been resolved. Why when she was out of pain did I make her take the medicine? I wanted to go deeper than the pain, to the root of the infection.

Many times once we feel a little better, we stop taking God's word for our health. And if we are not careful, the problem can come back.

Heed the Warnings

Some prescription bottles look like a rainbow with so many colorful warnings on the label. Have you seen the ones in bright orange and yellow and even red? There are warnings, and we need to heed the advice of the pharmacist.

Some labels will say not to take this medicine on an empty stomach, some will tell you not to crush the pill, some warning labels will tell you that you may become dizzy and to be careful if you plan to drive. If we do not obey the warning, it can affect the outcome and, sometimes it will hinder our healing. I went through such a time.

There is a very high rate of cancer in my mom's family. She was the youngest of nine children, and every one of my aunts and uncles had some form of cancer. My mom died from this horrible disease in 1979, and from that time on, I had to fight the fear of cancer.

Once while at a church service, the speaker mentioned that his parents had died of cancer, and he refused to allow the fear to torment his life. When the altar call was given at the end of his sermon, I ran up front to receive prayer. When the man of God laid hands on me, I received a beautiful deliverance from the spirit of fear.

Several weeks after this touch from God, I discovered a small lump in my left breast. I knew that this was a counterattack to try to steal what the Lord had just done for me only a few weeks ago. I made up my mind to fight the good fight of faith, to stand on the Word of God, and my husband agreed with me, and we prayed together for my healing.

As you read this, please do not imitate anyone else's walk with the Lord. I am all for going to the doctors, having regular checkups, and to work at being healthy. However, I was concerned that if I went to my doctor and got a negative report, the spirit of fear would once again torment my life. I believed God for my total healing, and I began to quote healing verses from the Bible and to thank God that by the stripes of Jesus I am healed. I didn't see any recovery, and the lump began to grow in size, but I just kept trusting and believing, so I thought.

After a good length of time had passed, my husband shared his concern for me with our daughter. My daughter came to see me with tears in her eyes, assuring me that she did not want me to die young like my mom. She wanted me to live a long life, see her married, and to be a grandmom to her future children. I began to cry out of her love for me and agreed to make an appointment with my gynecologist first thing in the morning.

I had a mammogram, and before I could finish dressing, there was a knock on the door that the doctors wanted to speak with me. This was no surprise to me as I was well aware of the large lump in my breast. Several doctors took me into a conference room and explained that they were very alarmed about the results of my test. They advised me to go into the hospital and have a biopsy at once. I told them they could schedule the procedure for tomorrow, and I went home with heaviness and disappointment in my heart.

I was believing, wasn't I? I was making my faith confession daily, wasn't I? Then why wasn't my healing appearing?

The next day, I had some of my ministry women at my home for a meeting, and I began to cry and asked them to pray for me. Something very strange happened next. One of the women laid her hands on me, and as she prayed, the Lord spoke. She asked the Lord to show me why the curse had come and then quoted a scripture that I had never heard—Proverbs 26:2: "As the bird by wandering, as the swallow by flying, so the curse causeless shall not come." My friend Shirley asked the Lord why this had come, and was there a cause that was hindering my healing? The curse, causeless, does not come; what did that mean? At the moment of her prayer, I felt that the Lord was speaking to my heart, and He said, "There is a cause that this curse has not be removed from you. It is because you are in sin."

I grew up a Roman Catholic and was taught to always confess my sin, and every night, have a prayer of contrition. I didn't always pray the prayer, but I tried to not practice sin. So what was this sin that had interfered with my faith and my confession. I was taken aback by the voice of the Lord, and I listened intently to what was to follow.

The sin was worry. Yes, you heard me right. The Lord said I was in the sin of worry, and how right He was. At that moment, I began to cry and confess that I was in sin, and my sin was the sin of worry. All the women who were praying for me began to pat my back as if to say "poor dear."

When I acknowledged my sin, the Lord miraculously healed me on the spot. The mass dissolved in my breast. Oh, how we rejoiced and praised God. Later that afternoon when I went for the biopsy, the lump was completely gone. Thank you, Jesus. And after all these years, I am still healthy, and I get my mammogram every year.

Some conditions require that medicine be taken every so many hours. I have a friend who sets his watch every four hours, and when the alarm goes off, he takes his medicine. It would be wonderful if we decided to take God's word as medicine for our flesh every four hours.

We wake in the morning and take Psalm 103:1–3 that tells us the Lord heals all our diseases as our first dose. Then at lunchtime, we apply Psalm 107:20: "He sent his word and healed them." After supper, we take 1 Peter 2:24: "Who his own self bare our sins in his own body on the tree, that we being dead to sins should live unto righteousness; by whose stripes ye were healed." And of course, before going to bed, we apply Exodus 15:26: "If thou wilt diligently hearken to the voice of the LORD thy God and wilt do that which is right in his sight, and wilt give ear to his commandments and keep all his statutes I will put none of these diseases upon thee which I have brought upon the Egyptians: for I am the LORD that healeth thee."

Now that I have shared all these truths from the natural realm, we need to put a spiritual application to all of these things.

First, make an appointment with the great physician. The above scripture in Exodus 15:26 introduces the Lord to us by His Hebrew name, which is Jehovah Rapha, "the Lord my physician." The good news is that he always has time to see you; he is never out of the office due to a surgery or away on vacation.

Second, wait on the Lord just as you would sit in the doctor's office. We must learn to wait on the Lord. Can you imagine someone pacing back and forth for an hour as they wait for their appointment? Not only do we wait, but we also practice patience and keep a calm spirit. Look at these wonderful promises: "It is good that a man should both hope and quietly wait" (Lam. 3:26), "I waited patiently for the LORD; and he inclined unto me, and heard my cry" (Ps. 40:1), and "they that wait upon the LORD shall renew their strength; they shall mount up with wings as eagles; they shall run, and not be weary; and they shall walk, and not faint" (Isa. 40:31).

Third, we need to examine ourselves as it says in 2 Corinthians 13:5, "Examine yourselves, whether ye be in the faith; prove your own selves." Many women have been spared from the late stages of breast cancer because they have been taught to do self-examination. We should examine ourselves as this verse says to see that we are in faith.

Fourth, receive the prescription from the Lord's Word. I remember a time I was angry at a lady, and when I was examining my heart, the perception that the Lord prescribed was not only to forgive her and ask for forgiveness for myself but to send her a fruit basket. Sometimes, it will cost you to have the script filled. But the benefits are wonderful. She and I were restored, and both of us walked in emotional health toward each other.

Fifth, take your medicine as directed. And when the meds get low, spend time once again with your great Physician.

Thank God for Jesus and His healing virtue. May it flow in your body, soul, and spirit.

6

STANDING FOR OUR CHILDREN

Have you ever seen the children's magazine called *Highlights*? In this magazine, they have several pictures that contain hidden images. There may be a winter scene, and under the picture, the caption will read find a candy cane, two pair of gloves, and a sled. My children really loved the adventure of finding all the hidden objects. And I must admit even as an adult many times before they came home from school, I had found all the items, but I never let on when they would get all excited because they saw a picture in a picture.

The Bible story I am about to open is really a picture in a picture. My prayer is that you will be able to see beyond just the surface to the deeper truths that this story represents. I am going to share the entire story and then begin to dialog some of what the Spirit of God has spoken to my heart.

This can be a source of great strength and insight for each of us to stand for those we love.

> There was a famine in the days of David three years, year after year and David enquired of the LORD and the LORD answered "It is for Saul and for his bloody house because he slew the Gibeonites." And the king called the Gibeonites and said unto them (now the Gibeonites were not of the children of Israel but of the remnant of the Amorites and the children of Israel had sworn unto them and Saul sought to slay them in his zeal to the children of Israel and Judah.) David said unto the Gibeonites "What shall I do for you? and wherewith shall I make the atonement that ye may bless the inheritance of the LORD?" And the Gibeonites said unto him "We will have no silver or gold of Saul nor of his house neither for us shalt thou kill any man in Israel. And he said "What ye shall say, that will I do for you." And they answered the king "The man that consumed us and that devised against us that we should be destroyed from remaining in any of the coasts of Israel, let seven men of his sons be delivered unto us and we will hang them up unto the LORD in Gibeah of Saul, whom the LORD did choose." And the king said "I will give them." But the king spared Mephibosheth, the son of Jonathan the son of Saul because of the LORD's oath that was between them, between David and Jonathan the son of Saul. But the king took the two sons of Rizpah the daughter of Aiah, whom she bare unto Saul, Armoni and Mephibosheth and

the five sons of Michal the daughter of Saul, whom she brought up for Adriel the son of Barzillai the Meholathite. And he delivered them into the hands of the Gibeonites and they hanged them in the hill before the LORD and they fell all seven together and were put to death in the days of harvest, in the first days, in the beginning of barley harvest. And Rizpah the daughter of Aiah took sackcloth and spread it for her upon the rock from the beginning of harvest until water dropped upon them out of heaven and suffered neither the birds of the air to rest on them by day nor the beasts of the field by night. And it was told David what Rizpah the daughter of Aiah the concubine of Saul, had done. And David went and took the bones of Saul and the bones of Jonathan his son from the men of Jabeshgilead which had stolen them from the street of Bethshan where the Philistines had hanged them, when the Philistines had slain Saul in Gilboa. (2 Samuel 21:1–12)

Who in the World are the Gibeonites?

This portion of scripture is very difficult and hard to understand—how seven innocent men were murdered, and King David allowed this tragedy to occur. I need to start at the very beginning.

There was a famine in the land, and the Bible says it lasted three years. As a matter of fact, the Bible repeats itself in verse 1 so that we can get the severity of the famine. There was a famine three years, year after year.

I have never experienced a famine or a drought in my lifetime, but there have been times when our water level was low, and our state issued a decree that we were not allowed to water our lawns or wash our cars due to the pending water shortage. There was a stiff fine for anyone who violated this warning. Can you even image no rain for three years?

David knew that God had promised to provide his blessings with an abundance of rain, and David also knew that if the heavens were shut up and a famine was in the land, something was seriously wrong.

David inquired of the Lord, and the Lord answered him and said that the famine was due to Saul's treatment of the Gibeonites. Before we can even begin to open this scripture and look at a woman named Rizpah, who stood on guard for her children, we must see why God was so angry at Saul and why did it matter if a pagan nation of the Gibeonites were killed.

A Binding Contract

Something had happened in the days of Joshua that must be fully understood for any of 2 Samuel chapter 21 to make sense. Here is the story:

> And it came to pass, when all the kings which were on this side Jordan, in the hills and in the valleys and in all the coasts of the great sea over against Lebanon heard thereof that they gathered themselves together to fight with Joshua and with Israel. When the inhabitants of Gibeon heard what Joshua had done unto Jericho and

to Ai they did work wilily and went and made as if they had been ambassadors and took old sacks upon their asses and wine bottles, old and rent and bound up; And old shoes and clouted upon their feet and old garments upon them and all the bread of their provision was dry and mouldy. And they went to Joshua unto the camp at Gilgal, and said unto him and to the men of Israel "We come from a far country: now therefore make ye a league with us." And the men of Israel said unto the Hivites "Peradventure ye dwell among us and how shall we make a league with you?" And they said unto Joshua "We are thy servants" and Joshua said unto them "Who are ye and from whence come ye?" And they said unto him "From a very far country thy servants are come because of the name of the LORD thy God: for we have heard the fame of him and all that he did. Our elders and all the inhabitants of our country spake to us saying "Take victuals with you for the journey and go to meet them and say unto them "We are your servants: therefore now make ye a league with us." "This our bread we took hot for our provision out of our houses on the day we came forth to go unto you but now, behold, it is dry, and it is mouldy and these bottles of wine, which we filled, were new and behold, they be rent and these our garments and our shoes are become old by reason of the very long journey." And the men took of their victuals and asked not counsel at the mouth of the LORD and Joshua made peace with them and made a league with them to let them live. And it came to pass at the end of three days that they heard that they were their neighbors and that they dwelt among them. And the children of Israel journeyed and came unto their cities on the third day. And the children of Israel smote them not because the princes of the congregation had sworn unto them by the LORD God of Israel. The princes said unto all the congregation "We have sworn unto them by the LORD God of Israel now therefore we may not touch them. This we will do to the, we will even let them live, lest wrath be upon us because of the oath which we sware unto them. And the princes said unto them "Let them live; but let them be hewers of wood and drawers of water unto all the congregation; as the princes had promised them." And Joshua called for them saying "Wherefore have ye beguiled us, saying, we are very far from you when ye dwell among us? Now therefore ye are cursed, and there shall none of you be freed from being bondmen and hewers of wood and drawers of water for the house of my God." And they answered Joshua and said "Because it was certainly told thy servants how that the LORD thy God commanded his servant Moses to give you all the land, and to destroy all the inhabitants of the land from before you therefore we were sore afraid of our lives because of you and have done this thing. And now, behold, we are in thine hand: as it seemeth good and right unto thee to do unto us, do. And so did he unto them and delivered them out of the hand of the children of Israel, that they slew them not. (Joshua 9:1–26, KJV)

Because of Joshua's great victory at Jericho and Ai, the Gibeonites were afraid of the army of Israel, and they didn't want to be destroyed, so they devised a deception that fooled Joshua and the men of God. They tricked them by their appearance. The one verse in this chapter that really caught my attention is verse 14, "And they sought not counsel of the Lord." I believe that God will keep us from being deceived if we only seek him. How many times have things looked one way, and then we find out that there is something different altogether going on.

Because Joshua didn't seek the counsel of God, he made a covenant of peace with these people and later found out he had been tricked and lied to. God then told Joshua, "Because you have made a league of agreement with them you cannot kill them and for all the generations they had to be protected. And they will supply the water and wood for the sanctuary."

King Saul began to kill the Gibeonites and to dishonor his covenant with them that was made by Joshua, God allowed the heavens to be closed according to His word in Deuteronomy 11:16–17, "Take heed to yourselves, that your heart be not deceived, and ye turn aside, and serve other gods, and worship them; And then the LORD's wrath be kindled against you, and he shut up the heaven, that there be no rain, and that the land yield not her fruit; and lest ye perish quickly from off the good land which the LORD giveth you." Because the agreement made with the

Gibeonites and Joshua was broken, there was no rain. God stopped up the heavens and got everyone's attention.

The Rage of Revenge

The Gibeonites could not be bought off or bribed; they said they don't want any of Saul's gold or silver. What they want is innocent blood shed for the innocent blood of their people whom Saul has killed. David consented to their appeal and allowed seven of Saul's sons to be killed.

Now we will meet a mother whose heart was broken. Her name is Rizpah, and both of her sons were killed. She was one of Saul's concubines and had little or no rights since she wasn't even his wife. After her sons were murdered, their naked bodies were impaled on poles where the fowls of the air and the beasts of the fields could devour their flesh. Please be aware that this happened in the Middle East, which is known for its hot and dry climate. The stench and decay must have been atrocious as the flesh was being ripped from the bodies of Saul's sons.

Now enter Rizpah, a woman who will stand in front of her sons, and have warfare like none other.

Remove the Sackcloth

The first thing we see about Rizpah is that she had sackcloth; this was a garment that was worn to show grief and sorrow. We don't wear such garments when we suffer loss, but we have a way of acknowledging death in our country.

When President Kennedy was assassinated, our entire nation went into mourning. My father wore a black armband over his shirt for several days. All of our state buildings' windows were covered with black cloth. Our flag was lowered to half-mast, and everyone could visibly see our grief. For a more current description, let me mention 9/11. After that tragedy, people by the hundreds brought flowers, photos, letters, stuffed animals, and all types of mementos to ground zero so that anyone in our country, even a foreigner, would know that we had suffered a loss.

Jacob is a great example of a man who wore sackcloth. In Genesis 37:34, when Jacob saw the evidence of Joseph's demise, we read, "Jacob rent his clothes and *put sackcloth upon his loins, and mourned* for his son many days" (emphasis added).

Mordecai is an example of wearing sackcloth in times of great injustice. The Jews were about to be killed, and he put on sackcloth to show his sorrow at the impending doom that was about to follow at the extinction of the Jewish nation.

> Mordecai rent his clothes and put on sackcloth with ashes and went out into the midst of the city and cried with a loud and a bitter cry; And came even before the king's gate, for none might enter into the king's gate clothed with sackcloth. And in every province, whithersoever the king's commandment and his decree came there was great

mourning among the Jews and fasting and weeping and wailing and many lay in sackcloth and ashes. So Esther's maids and her chamberlains came and told it her. Then was the queen exceedingly grieved and she sent raiment to clothe Mordecai and to take away his sackcloth from him but he received it not. (Esther 4:1–4)

Now we know from the book of Esther that God intervened, and the nation was saved. But even when asked to remove his sackcloth, Mordecai wouldn't do it.

Stand Upon the Rock

From these two thoughts and scriptures, we can see that Rizpah had every right to wear sackcloth. She was in sorrow and grief at the death of her two sons, and it was a great injustice; however, she did something we need to do.

We need to follow Rizpah's example. She took off the sackcloth and laid it on the rock. Too many of us can't seem to let go of our pain, sorrow, and disappointment; but we must go to Jesus, the rock of our salvation, and lay it down. David gave us examples in the book of Psalms (KJV):

The LORD is my rock and my fortress, and my deliverer; my God, my strength, in whom I will trust; my buckler, and the horn of my salvation, and my high tower. (18:2)

For in the time of trouble he shall hide me in his pavilion: in the secret of his tabernacle shall he hide me; he shall set me up upon a rock. (27:5)

But the LORD is my defense and my God is the rock of my refuge. (94:22)

Birds of the Air

Rizpah would not let a bird of the air touch the body of her sons. I can't even begin to imagine the vultures and crows and all the birds that would want to feast on their flesh. I saw the movie *The Birds* years ago and wouldn't go into a phone booth for many years because that movie had scared me.

What do the birds or fowls of the air represent in this picture within a picture? Two things stand out to me in the Bible, and I believe these are just two of the assignments of the birds of the air: The first is that they have been sent to stop blood covenant. In Genesis chapter 15, God is about to cut blood covenant with Abram, and after the animals were cut into two pieces for the covenant, the birds came down to devour the sacrifice, and Abram did something identical to Rizpah. "And when the fowls came down upon the carcasses, Abram drove them away" (15:11).

The second thing that the fowls of the air represent is found in the New Testament. This is a very well-known story about a sower who sowed seed, and as soon as the seed was sown, the birds of the air came to remove the seed.

The story is told in Matthew 13, Mark 4, and Luke 8, and in each of these accounts, we can gleam more insight as to the birds of the air.

Seeds are sown, and the birds of the air came and devoured them. Jesus was asked to explain this parable. Let's look at the definition of the birds of the air from the book of Matthew: "When any one heareth the word of the kingdom, and understandeth it not, then cometh the wicked one and catcheth away that which was sown in his heart. This is he which received seed by the way side" (Matt. 13:19). Jesus called the birds of the air the wicked one.

In Mark 4:15, it says, "And these are they by the way side, where the word is sown but when they have heard, Satan cometh immediately and taketh away the word that was sown in their hearts." Now we know that the wicked one is Satan. And finally, in Luke 8:12: "Those by the way side are they that hear; then cometh the devil and taketh away the word out of their hearts, lest they should believe and be saved." So we see that the wicked one is Satan, also called the devil, and he wants to stop us from understanding the Word of God. However, like Rizpah, we can drive back the birds of the air.

The Beast Within

The next thing that Rizpah did was that she would not allow a beast of the night to touch her sons. I don't know what types of animals are conducive to her native homeland, and

I remember spending a great deal of time trying to study all the different beasts in the scriptures. I was frustrated because I could not understand what this verse was saying to me as a parent who wanted to stand for my children and grandchildren. Finally, I just looked up the word *beast* and to my surprise one of the definitions is any uncontrolled or undisciplined appetite. We all have things in our lives, as well as in our children's lives, that could use more discipline and control.

We Need a Downpour

Rizpah stood until the rains came. We don't know how long she stood on the rock with the sackcloth at her feet as she drove back birds and the beasts, but the Bible said she did this in the beginning of the barley harvest till the rains came. Bible scholars say that the beginning of the barley harvest happens in the month of April, and the rains don't come till early fall. I cannot set any amount of time to her protecting the bodies of her boys, but be assured she stood many days till the rain came.

What in the scripture does the rain represent? Just two thoughts I want to share with you, these two aspects of God are what I pray over my children: First, in Hosea 6:1–3, His presence is compared to the rains.

> Come, and let us return unto the LORD: for he hath torn, and he will heal us; he hath smitten, and he will bind us up. After two days will he revive us: in

the third day he will raise us up, and we shall live in his sight. Then shall we know, if we follow on to know the LORD: his going forth is prepared as the morning; and he shall come unto us as the rain, as the latter and former rain unto the earth.

Don't we all need His presence in our lives?

The second thing that rain represents in His Word is in Deuteronomy 32:1–3: "Give ear, O ye heavens, and I will speak and hear O earth, the words of my mouth. My doctrine shall drop as the rain; my speech shall distil as the dew, as the small rain upon the tender herb, and as the showers upon the grass: Because I will publish the name of the LORD: ascribe ye greatness unto our God."

And we read in Isaiah 55:8–11:

For my thoughts are not your thoughts, neither are your ways my ways, saith the LORD. For as the heavens are higher than the earth so are my ways higher than your ways and my thoughts than your thoughts. For as the rain cometh down, and the snow from heaven, and returneth not thither, but watereth the earth, and maketh it bring forth and bud, that it may give seed to the sower, and bread to the eater: So shall my word be that goeth forth out of my mouth: it shall not return unto me void, but it shall accomplish that which I please, and it shall prosper in the thing whereto I sent it.

When you stand to drive away the birds and the beasts, and you call for the rains of God, what we are calling for in the lives of our loved ones is more of God's presence and more of His Word. Oh, Lord, let it rain.

All We Need to See is a Little Cloud

Just because we pray and take our stand doesn't guarantee immediate results; we need to be prepared to stand as long as it takes till the rains come. There is a great example in the life of Elijah I want to share. It had not rained in three years, and God had told his prophet that he was about to send the rains.

> And Elijah said unto Ahab, Get thee up, eat and drink; for there is a sound of abundance of rain. So Ahab went up to eat and to drink. And Elijah went up to the top of Carmel; and he cast himself down upon the earth, and put his face between his knees, And said to his servant, Go up now, look toward the sea. And he went up, and looked, and said, There is nothing. And he said, Go again seven times. And it came to pass at the seventh time, that he said, Behold, there ariseth a little cloud out of the sea, like a man's hand. And he said, Go up, say unto Ahab, Prepare thy chariot, and get thee down that the rain stop thee not. And it came to pass in the mean while, that the heaven was black with clouds and wind, and there was a great rain. And Ahab rode, and went to Jezreel. (1 Kings 18:41–45, KJV)

Please note that even before he prayed for the rain, he heard the sound of an abundance of rain (verse 41). We need to hear the sound of the abundance of rain from the Spirit of God even before the rainfall.

The next thing Elijah did was pray, and then after the sound and the seeking, he sent his servant—not just once or twice, but seven times—until there was only a cloud the size of a man's fist. But it was enough to move Elijah to tell the king to move quickly before the downfall. We need to stay consistent and pray until the rains come.

King David heard about what Rizpah did for her sons, and he had them taken down and buried.

In closing this chapter, I want to share some details with what the name *Rizpah* means: a hot coal. Her sons names were Armoni and Mephibosheth. The name *Armoni* means one who belongs in a palace and *Mephibosheth* is one who destroys shame.

Never forget that Jesus came to destroy all sin and shame in our lives as well as the lives of our children and grandchildren. Because Jesus is the King of kings, we have a right to enter into the palace and fellowship with him.

My prayer is that each of us will stand on Jesus our rock with the sackcloth at his feet, and we will drive back the birds and the beast until the rain of His presence and His Word refreshes each of us.

7

THORNS IN THE FLESH ARE A MESS

In this chapter, I want to tackle a portion of scripture that has been misunderstood by many wonderful believers. Jesus told us if we don't understand the scriptures, then the enemy comes to remove the word from our hearts. There are times that our traditions have hindered us from understanding or caused us to misinterpret a portion of His word.

Each of us will have to make a decision to allow the Holy Spirit to speak truth into our hearts. The Bible has a great deal to say about traditions. Let's look at some of the warnings in the New Testament, starting in Mark 7:6–13:

> He answered and said unto them "Well hath Esaias prophesied of you hypocrites as it is written 'This people honored me with their lips but their heart is far from me. Howbeit in vain do they worship me, teaching for doctrines the commandments of

men.' For laying aside the commandment of God ye hold the tradition of men, as the washing of pots and cups and many other such like things ye do." And he said unto them 'Full well ye reject the commandment of God, that ye may keep your own tradition. For Moses said, 'Honor thy father and thy mother and who so curses father or mother, let him die the death.' But ye say 'If a man shall say to his father or mother it is Corbin, that is to say, a gift, by whatsoever thou mightiest be profited by me; he shall be free.' And ye suffer him no more to do ought for his father or his mother making the word of God of none effect through your tradition, which ye have delivered and many such like things do ye."

There is a pattern that we must look at from these verses: First, in verse 7, Jesus tells them that what they are being taught is the commandments of men, and they are receiving it as a doctrine. The second thing that happens is in verse 8, where they lay aside the commandments of God so that they can hold on to their own traditions. Then by the time we get to verse 9, the third thing that happens is they have rejected the Word of God so they can keep their own tradition. The fourth and final thing that happens is in verse 13, and it is such a serious verse that I pray you and I don't overlook the damage that traditions of men can do. When we hold our traditions over the Word of God, we make the Bible void of its power to perform in our lives.

Making the Word of God to no effect is how the King James Version puts Mark 7:13. I want us to look at several versions so we can receive the full impact of what God is saying to us. The New International Version: "Thus you *nullify* the word of God by your tradition that you have handed down. And you do many things like that" (emphasis added). The definition of *nullify* is to make something invalid or ineffective, to cancel something out. From the thesaurus, we find words such as *annul*, *abolish*, *quash*, and *reverse*.

The New American Standard version says, "Thus *invalidating* the word of God by your tradition which you have handed down and you do many things such as that" (emphasis added). The definition of the word *invalid* is to deprive something of its legal force or value by failing to comply with some terms and conditions, to make something worthless.

The Amplified Bible puts it this way, "Thus you are nullifying and making void and of no effect the authority of the Word of God through your tradition, which you [in turn] hand on. And many things of this kind you are doing."

Remember, it's the commandments of men and their traditions that cause the word to be ineffective in our lives. Just look at what the commandments of men can do. Paul, writing a letter to Titus, penned, "Not giving heed to Jewish fables and commandments of men that turn from the truth" (Tit. 1:14, KJV). And then we have Paul writing to the Colossians, "Beware lest any man spoil you through philosophy and vain deceit, after the tradition of men, after the rudiments of the world and not after Christ" (Col. 2:8, KJV). Traditions can make the Word of God powerless; it can turn you from the truth, and as it says in Colossians 2:8, it can spoil you.

The tradition of men that I want to bring to light is namely Paul's thorn. We will delve into the complete story of his thorn, which is found in the book of 2 Corinthians; however, before I get too detailed, I must share with you my first introduction to the phrase "Paul's thorn in the flesh."

When I was a young Christian, I attended a weekly Bible study taught by my pastor's wife. It was a wonderful study with good fellowship and carried a strong anointing. One Tuesday morning, a lady came in with a large white bandage on her hand. Of course, everyone wanted to know what had happened to her. She told us that morning she was frying bacon for her children's breakfast, and some of the hot grease hit her hand, causing a very serious burn and blister. She cleansed the burn and came to church to ask us to pray for her healing.

As she stood in front of our group, my pastor's wife said that she wasn't sure if this burn would be healed when we pray because this could be like Paul's thorn. There it is again, that phrase "Paul's thorn." What in the world was his thorn? I had heard of the apostle Paul, but I never heard about a thorn, and I couldn't understand why it might not be God's will to heal her.

If you have ever suffered from a burn, you know how very painful they can be. So what does this thorn in the flesh have to do with her not being healed? I could hardly wait for the study to end so I could go home and look up this mysterious thorn.

Here's what I read in 2 Corinthians 12:1–11:

> It is not expedient for me doubtless to glory. I will come to visions and revelations of the Lord. I knew a man in Christ above fourteen years ago (whether in the body, I cannot tell; or whether out of the body, I cannot tell: God knoweth) such an one caught up to the third heaven. And I knew such a man, (whether in the body, or out of the body, I cannot tell: God knoweth) how that he was caught up into paradise and heard unspeakable words, which it is not lawful for a man to utter. Of such an one will I glory: yet of myself I will not glory but in mine infirmities. For though I would desire to glory, I shall not be a fool for I will say the truth but now I forbear, lest any man should think of me above that which he seeth me to be or that he heareth of me. And lest I should be exalted above measure through the abundance of the revelations, there was given to me a thorn in the flesh, the messenger of Satan to buffet me, lest I should be exalted above measure. For this thing I besought the Lord thrice that it might depart from me. And he said unto me "My grace is sufficient for thee for my strength is made perfect in weakness." Most gladly therefore will I rather glory

in my infirmities that the power of Christ may rest upon me. Therefore I take pleasure in infirmities, in reproaches, in necessities, in persecutions, in distresses for Christ's sake: for when I am weak, then am I strong. I am become a fool in glorying, ye have compelled me, for I ought to have been commended of you for in nothing am I behind the very chiefest apostles, though I be nothing.

I read and reread this portion, trying to understand why or how this story would interfere with us praying for our friend. It wasn't until I talked with other people and found out what had been taught in many churches that I was able to understand my pastor's wife heart that day.

This is what has been taught by traditions of men: that God gave Paul a thorn in his flesh, and even though he prayed three times for God to remove it, God said no and would not heal him because he needed to have some infirmity in his flesh to keep him humble to depend upon God. This entire paragraph is incorrect, and with the Holy Spirit's help and anointing, I want to dispel false doctrine and help each of us to know what his thorn was.

Changing Metaphors

In every generation, we have different slang, sayings, and cute phrases that are known to us in that time period. Let me give you an example: in the '60s, we had the love children, or hippies, as they were known. They dressed different than most of society, and they definitely spoke different than the mainstream.

Let's say a hippie wanted money from his father, and he decided to leave him a note, which would read as "Hey there bebop daddy O, I need some dough, my cars a lemon, leave the dough on the table. Wow, groovy like thanks, man. Yea!"

Now we are going to bury this letter for one thousand years; there are no tape recorders or videos from this time and era, and the letter is unearthed. If you never heard of a love child or the Beatnik Generation, you would not be able to comprehend the true meaning of the letter even though you could read it. Only after a lesson in the culture and times would you be able to make sense of such a letter. After you were educated in this movement, you would come to know that dough wasn't about bread or flour or yeast; dough was cold hard cash. And it almost goes without saying that a car can't be a lemon. What it means is his car was inferior or as another slang saying goes, my car is a dud.

This is also a truth that we must apply to the Bible; we need to know the culture, times, and customs to fully understand scriptures, such as Paul's thorn.

Just in my day alone, words have come to have much different meanings. As a preteen, my friends and I would all do Coke, not drugs, but a soda at the fountain in the drugstore downtown. Pot was something you cooked in, and grass was something you cut. We have many of our own metaphors: how about he has ice water in his veins, or I would cut off my right arm for you, or so and so is a pain in my neck, or just kick it to the curb.

Do you see the difference? Well, so it is with this portion of the Bible.

Who Would Glory in Infirmities?

I will glory in my infirmities? One problem is that when we hear the word *infirmities*, we think of sickness. Yet in the Bible, that word is also translated weakness. Because we have infirmaries, which are hospitals and ERs, we associate this word with illness.

This word must be clearly defined before you and I can fully understand Paul's thorn.

> Jesus came into Peter's house where he saw his wife's mother laid up and sick with fever and he touched her hand and the fever left her and she rose up and ministered to them. When the even was come, they brought unto him many that were possessed with devils and he cast out the spirits with his word and healed all that were sick that it might be fulfilled which was spoken by Esaias the prophet, saying "Himself took our infirmities and bare our sicknesses." (Matthew 8:14–17)

Jesus took our infirmities and bore our sickness, so we can see that these two things are different.

In Paul's discourse on his thorn, he never said it was illness or sickness; as a matter of fact, he listed his infirmities in which he gloried in 2 Corinthians 11:23–30.

> Are they ministers of Christ? I am more; in labors more abundant, in stripes above measure, in prisons more frequent, in deaths oft. Of the Jews five times received I forty stripes save one. Thrice was I beaten with rods, once was I stoned, thrice I suffered shipwreck, a night and a day I have been in the deep. In journeying often in perils of waters, in perils of robbers, in perils by mine own countrymen, in perils by the heathen, in perils in the city, in perils in the wilderness, in perils in the sea, in perils among false brethren. In weariness and painfulness, in watching's often, in hunger and thirst, in fasting often, in cold and nakedness. Beside those things that are without, that which cometh upon me daily is the care of all the churches. Who is weak and I am not weak? Who is offended and I burn not? If I must needs glory I will glory of the things which concern mine infirmities.

It is of note that in this extensive list, we fail to see *sickness*. These are the list of his infirmities, and personal illness is not listed.

Another powerful verse that will help us understand this is Romans 8:26: "Likewise the Spirit also helpeth our infirmities for we know not what we should pray for as we ought but the Spirit itself maketh intercession for us with groanings which cannot be uttered." Here we see that in our weakness, the Holy Spirit helps us pray. Infirmities cannot be illness because how could God's spirit in us get sick?

2 Corinthians 12:9 will give us even more insight: "And he said unto me 'My grace is sufficient for thee for my strength is made perfect in weakness. Most gladly therefore will I rather glory in my infirmities that the power of Christ may rest upon me.'" The Greek word *weakness* and the word *infirmities* in this verse are the same word. So when we see the word infirmities, we need to consider the text in which it appears. All of us have weakness that the enemy would like to attack.

There are times in the New Testament that an infirmity is sickness and disease as it is in Luke 5:15: "But so much the more went there a fame abroad of him and great multitudes came together to hear and to be healed by him of their infirmities."

So What is the Thorn?

One thing we must remember is that Paul knew the Old Testament and the people that this letter was written to. He also knew the Bible and the customs of the day. We are told that through two or three witnesses, everything will be established; Jesus quoted it from the Old Testament, and even Paul used this principle (Matt. 18:16, 2 Cor. 13:1). Using four witnesses from the Old Testament, this thorn in Paul's flesh will be revealed.

The Thorn was Not from God

First, in 2 Corinthians 12:7: "And lest I should be exalted above measure through the abundance of the revelations, there was given to me a thorn in the flesh, the messenger of Satan to buffet me, lest I should be exalted above measure." Please look at what God is saying; it was the messenger of Satan. Why do we say God gave him this thorn when the Bible says it was from Satan?

Here we go on our witness search.

> And ye shall divide the land by lot for an inheritance among your families: and to the more ye shall give the more inheritance and to the fewer ye shall give the less inheritance: every man's inheritance shall be in the place where his lot falleth according to the tribes of your fathers ye shall inherit. But if ye will not drive out the inhabitants of the land from before you then it shall come to pass that those which ye let remain of them shall be pricks in your eyes, and *thorns in your sides* and shall vex you in the land wherein ye dwell. (Numbers 33:54–55; emphasis added)

This scripture from the book of Numbers actually uses almost the identical terminology, "thorns in your sides." You will notice from this scripture that it has nothing to do with sickness or disease. What this verse is dealing with is the unsaved pagan people of the day whom they were to drive out of their land, and if they didn't remove these people, they would be thorns in their sides.

Witness number 2 in Joshua 23:13: "Know for a certainty that the LORD your God will no more drive out any of these nations from before you but they shall be snares and traps unto you, and scourges in your sides and *thorns in your eyes* until ye perish from off this good land which the LORD your God hath given you" (emphasis added). Once again, no reference to illness. These nations that were to be driven out will become thorns in your eyes and scourges in your sides.

Witness number 3 in Judges 2:1–3: "And an angel of the LORD came up from Gilgal to Bochim and said "I made you to go up out of Egypt and have brought you unto the land which I sware unto your fathers and I said I will never break my covenant with you. And ye shall make no league with the inhabitants of this land; ye shall throw down their altars but ye have not obeyed my voice, why have ye done this? Wherefore I also said, I will not drive them out from before you; but they shall be as thorns in your sides, and their gods shall be a snare unto you." There it is again, thorns in your side.

Let's look at the fourth and final witness in 2 Samuel 23:1–5: "Now these be the last words of David. David the son of Jesse said, and the man who was raised up on high, the anointed of the God of Jacob, and the sweet psalmist of Israel, said 'The Spirit of the LORD spoke by me and his word was in my tongue.'" The God of Israel said, the Rock of Israel spoke to me, "He that rules over men must be just, ruling in the fear of God. He shall be as the light of the morning when the sun rises, even a morning without clouds, as the tender grass springing out of the earth by clear shining after rain. Although my house be not so with God yet he hath made with me an everlasting covenant, ordered in all things and sure for this is all my salvation and all my desire, although he make it not to grow. But the sons of Belial shall be all of them as thorns thrust away because they cannot be taken with hands."

In every one of the four witnesses that has been used from the Bible, not once did it remotely deal with any type of illness. Therefore, we must let the Bible speak to us as to what the thorn really was.

The thorn in Paul's flesh was a messenger of Satan; it was the unsaved pagan people and nations that were to be driven out. King David said that the sons of Belial were thorns. This title Belial is in our New Testament—and again—no reference to any type of physical problem.

Paul wrote to the Corinthians the connection of believers and nonbelievers and the complications a union of the two would cause. "Be ye not unequally yoked together with unbelievers for what fellowship hath righteousness with unrighteousness? And what communion hath light with darkness? And what concord hath Christ with Belial? Or what part hath he that believeth with an infidel? And what agreement hath the temple of God with idols? For ye are the temple of the living God; as God hath said, 'I will dwell in them and walk in them and I will be their God and they shall be my people.'" (2 Cor. 6:14–16, KJV)

Belial represents the devil or Satan, and David said the sons of Belial were thorns. Notice sons of Belial seems very similar to the messenger of Satan. This thorn was from Satan; it was the persecution that was inflicted on Paul every time he preached Christ, by the unsaved.

Three Times I Asked

Paul asked the Lord to remove the thorn; God never did say no, as so many teach. God told Paul that his grace was sufficient. Now that we know the thorn was from Satan, we can understand why God just didn't remove every obstacle.

Remember, God had given believers authority over all the works of the devil. We can read it in Luke 10:19: "Behold, I give unto you power to tread on serpents and scorpions and over all the power of the enemy and nothing shall by any means hurt you." And James wrote: "Submit yourselves therefore to God. Resist the devil and he will flee from you" (Jam. 4:7, KJV).

More Than a Conqueror

We tend to teach that this thorn that was given to Paul lasted a lifetime. However, that doesn't agree with what the apostle Paul tells us. I often tell people who believe the thorn was a sickness that we should be so sick; Paul made many missionary journeys and wrote about one-third of the New Testament. I wonder how someone so afflicted in his body could accomplish so much.

Paul didn't allow the thorns to stop him; he has stress, but God's grace truly did free him from all the messengers of Satan. Paul wrote: "Persecutions, afflictions, which came unto me at Antioch, at Iconium, at Lystra; what persecutions I endured: but out of them all the Lord delivered me" (2 Tim. 3:11, KJV).

Paul fought a good fight; he kept his faith and lived to be a good age. He wrote in a letter to Timothy: "For I am now ready to be offered and the time of my departure is at hand. I have fought a good fight, I have finished my course, I have kept the faith: Henceforth there is laid up for me a crown of righteousness which the Lord, the righteous judge, shall give me at that day: and not to me only but unto all them also that love his appearing" (2 Tim. 4:6–8, KJ).

And he wrote to Philemon in chapter 1 verse 9: "Yet for love's sake I rather beseech thee, being such a one as Paul the aged and now also a prisoner of Jesus Christ. Paul was a prisoner of Jesus, not of the wicked one."

We all have thorns from the enemy; but we must, like Paul, depend on the grace of God to overcome them all.

8

LIVING WITH A LIMP

All of us have been hurt or wounded at one time or another. It is very hard to live your life and never be offended or disappointed. There is a story in the Old Testament that I have come to love, and it has brought countless healings in my heart and life, and I am so delighted to share this with you.

First, I need to share some background and to lay some foundation to this incredible event in the life of a young man named Mephibosheth.

A Friend Loveth at All Times

I trust that you have heard of the first king of Israel whose name was Saul. Saul faced many challenges; however, I think the most well-known of them all was when he and his army were faced with the giant named Goliath. For forty days and nights, Goliath verbally attacked the God of the Israelites. A young boy named David had been sent to the battlefield to provide food for his three elder brothers who were in Saul's army. As David approaches with provisions, he overhears the reproach to the name of the Lord and says that with God's help, he will silence the voice of the enemy. This is one of the most loved and well-known stories in the Bible.

With faith and a sling, David slays the giant Goliath and becomes a hero and is then called into the tent of King Saul. We can read it in 1 Samuel 17:57–58: "And as David returned from the slaughter of the Philistine, Abner took him and brought him before Saul with the head of the Philistine in his hand. And Saul said to him, whose son art thou, thou young man? And David answered, 'I am the son of thy servant Jesse the Bethlehemite.'"

> And it came to pass, when he had made an end of speaking unto Saul that the soul of Jonathan (Saul's son) was knit with the soul of David and Jonathan loved him as his own soul. And Saul took him that day, and would let him go no more home to his father's house. Then Jonathan and David made a covenant, because he loved him as his own soul. And Jonathan stripped himself of the robe that was upon him, and gave it to David and his garments, even to his sword and to his bow and to his girdle. And David went out whithersoever Saul sent him and behaved himself wisely and Saul set him over the men of war and he was accepted in the sight of all the people and also in the sight of Saul's servants. (1 Sam. 18:1–5, KJV)

A Godly Soul Tie

Jonathan was the son of King Saul, and the Bible says that his soul was knit to the soul of David and that they loved each other. At this point before I begin to show you their devoted friendship, I must address a disturbing distortion of scripture, and that is what some have said that David and Jonathan were lovers and that they were homosexuals. Nothing could be further from the truth.

David and Jonathan were men of God and not in love with each other in the sense that some would like us to believe. They made a covenant, which was honored by God, and their relationship was wholly devoted to the service of God and each other. This is a biblical example of what I would term a godly soul tie. We have had much teaching in the church on ungodly soul ties, yet, in this example we see God bringing together two men who honored the covenant.

Let me mention just a few godly soul ties in the scripture: Naomi and Ruth, Paul and Barnabas, Timothy and Silas, Lois and Eunice. They are just a few of the people God put together.

David and Jonathan have entered into a binding covenant, but King Saul becomes jealous of David's fame and tries to kill him; all the people were praising the hero of Israel, David became the captain of Saul's army. Can you imagine your father wants to kill your best friend? Saul made several unsuccessful attempts to kill David, and David was trying to communicate with Jonathan that his father was his enemy, but Jonathan couldn't believe it—it just wasn't getting through.

Finally, David came up with a plan to show his friend Saul's heart. There was a feast Saul hosted, and David's plan was to be absent, and if Saul gets angry because David wasn't there then maybe his son's eyes would be opened. For more details you can read 1 Samuel 20. Well Saul goes ballistic, and now the eyes of Jonathan are opened, and he sees that his own father hates his best friend.

Come Out, Come Out Wherever You Are!

Jonathan had a plan: if David was wrong and Saul's heart wasn't evil against David, he would practice his archery in a field with David hiding behind a bale of hay nearby. If he shot an arrow nearby, David would know he was safe and could come out of hiding. But if Jonathan shot the arrow far away, then David would know he had to run for his life, and it wasn't safe for him to be there.

Jonathan shot his arrow far away as a signal to David, and then he had his servant go and retrieve the arrow. The story continues in 1 Samuel 20:41–42:

> And as soon as the lad was gone, David arose out of a place toward the south and fell on his face to the ground and bowed himself three times and they kissed one another and wept one with another until David exceeded. And Jonathan said to David, "Go in peace, forasmuch as we have sworn both of

us in the name of the LORD saying 'The LORD be between me and thee and between my seed and thy seed forever.'" And he arose and departed and Jonathan went into the city.

They knew that they may never see each other again, so their friendship and promises were now extended to their children and their grandchildren.

A Double Tragedy

Moving to 2 Samuel 1:1–4, there's more:

> Now it came to pass after the death of Saul, when David was returned from the slaughter of the Amalekites and David had abode two days in Ziklag it came even to pass on the third day, that, behold, a man came out of the camp from Saul with his clothes rent and earth upon his head and so it was when he came to David that he fell to the earth and did obeisance. And David said unto him "from whence comest thou?" And he said unto him "Out of the camp of Israel am I escaped and David said unto him "How went the matter? I pray thee, tell me." And he answered that the people are fled from the battle and many of the people also are fallen and dead and Saul and Jonathan his son are dead also.

Saul and Jonathan died in the battle. What a terrible thing to hear that a father and his son both were killed on the same day. David went into mourning for King Saul as well as for Jonathan, his closest friend.

Well, there is another tragedy that happened at about the same time, and this accident happened to Jonathan's son.

Kill All the Male Children

There are some customs and traditions that we need to understand. In those days when you conquered a city, the first thing you would do is kill the king. He would be paraded in the streets, humiliated and dethroned then killed in a torturous way. The order would be issued from the new ruling king to kill all the males in his family line; that way, no one could claim the right to the throne but him. No brother, uncle, son, father, or grandfather could question your authority. This event led to Jonathan's son being injured.

In those times, they didn't have maternity and childcare wards in hospitals like we do today. What was common was midwives—women who would come to your home and help deliver your baby; they were also called nurses. Many would stay on and be the child's caretaker. Jonathan's son had such a nurse in his life. We don't know her name, but when she heard of the battle and the death of Saul and his son, she knew that this little boy was in harm's way.

Accidents Happen

"And Jonathan, Saul's son, had a son that was lame of his feet. He was five years old when the tidings came of Saul and Jonathan out of Jezreel and his nurse took him up and fled and it came to pass as she made haste to flee that he fell and became lame. And his name was Mephiboseth" (2 Sam. 4:4, KJV). This nurse had nothing but good intentions for this little five-year-old boy. She wanted to run and take him to a safe place, but something dreadful happened—she dropped him. As a result of this accident, he became a cripple for life. The Bible said he was lame in both his feet.

The word lame means is to be stricken or smitten. The word *stricken* is defined as deeply or badly affected, to be wounded or to suffer. *Smitten* means that someone else has caused this affliction. She never meant to hurt him, but he became a cripple because someone dropped him in his childhood.

Crippled Because Someone Dropped You

So many of us have had childhood injuries that last a lifetime, similar to Mephibosheth. When the person you trust to protect you drops you, it can do lasting damage. One of the things that the Lord has so beautifully done in my life is to help me forgive those people who dropped me.

My father had a serious problem with alcohol, and when he was drunk, he would beat my brothers. I do not think my parents ever realized the damage they did to me as an innocent bystander trying to understand rage and violence that crippled me well into my adult life. Fortunately, Jesus has healed many painful memories and events in my life that caused me to live with a crippling "limp." I cannot undo the pain or the memories, but I can go to the Lord for emotional healing in accidents where I was dropped by someone who should have protected me.

His nurse surely never meant to harm him. How many of us as parents wish we could undo some of the damage we did to our children? The only real solution is to receive forgiveness and, if at all possible, ask your children to forgive you. I have gone to my son and daughter many times since the Lord opened up this teaching to me on Mephibosheth and told them I am sorry for any pain, hurt, or injury I caused them.

Called by a King

Let me share with you a powerful chapter of redemption and restoration that happens in the life of a little boy who was crippled. Many years have gone by since his childhood injury, David is now the king of Israel, and he has never forgotten his promise and pledge to Jonathan.

> David asked "Is there anyone still left of the house of Saul to whom I can show kindness for Jonathan's sake?" Now there was a servant of Saul's household named Ziba. They called him to appear before David, and the king said to him, "Are you Ziba?" "Your servant" he replied. The king asked, "Is there no one still left of the house of Saul to whom I can show God's kindness?" Ziba answered

the king "There is still a son of Jonathan; he is crippled in both feet." "Where is he?" the king asked. Ziba answered "He is at the house of Machir son of Ammiel in Lo Debar." So King David had him brought from Lo Debar, from the house of Makir son of Ammiel. When Mephibosheth son of Jonathan, the son of Saul, came to David he bowed down to pay him honor. David said, "Mephibosheth!" "Your servant" he replied. "Don't be afraid" David said to him "for I will surely show you kindness for the sake of your father Jonathan. I will restore to you all the land that belonged to your grandfather Saul and you will always eat at my table." Mephibosheth bowed down and said "What is your servant that you should notice a dead dog like me?" Then the king summoned Ziba, Saul's servant, and said to him "I have given your master's grandson everything that belonged to Saul and his family. You and your sons and your servants are to farm the land for him and bring in the crops, so that your master's grandson may be provided for. And Mephibosheth, grandson of your master, will always eat at my table." (Ziba had fifteen sons and twenty servants) Then Ziba said to the king "Your servant will do whatever my lord the king commands his servant to do." So Mephibosheth ate at David's table like one of the king's sons. Mephibosheth had a young son named Micha and all the members of Ziba's household were servants of Mephibosheth. And Mephibosheth lived in Jerusalem because he

> always ate at the king's table and he was crippled in
> both feet. (2 Samuel 9:1–13)

As this chapter opens, we see David ask about the family of Saul and his dear friend Jonathan. As soon as David finds out about Jonathan's son, he sends for him. He may be a cripple, but he was called for by a king.

Of course, this should speak volumes about all of our lives that no matter what crippling events occurred, we have a king, and He has called for us. Jesus called for me in 1974, and once I met the king, I was able to learn to live even though I had crippling memories. What a wonderful Savior and Lord and King Jesus is.

Compensated to the Fullest

David had Mephibosheth brought out of the house of Machir from the town of Lo-debar. The name *Lo-debar* means a place of dryness without any pasture. Here we see the grandson of the first king of a great nation living in a dry place of emptiness. Just like the enemy wants to keep us crippled and in a dry wasted place with a fractured life. Jesus our king has come to give us life and life abundantly; we must leave Lo-debar and answer the call. "'Don't be afraid' David said to him 'for I will surely show you kindness for the sake of your father Jonathan. I will restore to you all the land that belonged to your grandfather Saul and you will always eat at my table.'" (2 Sam. 9:7).

Everything that belonged to his father and his father's kingdom was resorted to Mephibosheth. And that is what the father does for us when we come to his table.

Covered at the King's Table

Think with me for a moment, what happens to your feet and legs when you sit at a table? They are covered and concealed and out of sight. Once we sit at the table with the Lord, he covers all the things in our lives that have broken us. You would have to pull your chair out and away from the covering in order to see your infirmities.

Thank God, all of our sins are covered, and we must remain seated in his presence to overcome painful events in our lives.

Communion with His King

"As for Mephibosheth" said the king "he shall eat at my table as one of the king's sons" (2 Sam. 9:11b). Jesus has made us his sons and daughters, look at this wonderful verse: "But as many as received him, to them gave the power to become the sons of God, even to them that believe on his name" (John 1:12, KJV).

Once you and I have received him, He gives us the power to become sons of God because we believe in his name. Please do not let the gender bother you—in the Bible, I am called a son of God, and my gender is female. In the book of Revelation, we are called the bride of Christ, and that would include men.

There was a time when they sat down to eat the most important thing at the meal, was fellowship or, another way to put it, communion. But even though he was royalty and called by a king and compensated and had communion as a family member, the damage that was done could not be reversed: "Mephibosheth dwelt in Jerusalem: for he did eat continually at the king's table and was lame on both his feet" (2 Sam. 9:13).

His injury was not removed. Since our past cannot be undone, we need to stay at the table and look at the king and not focus on our past wounds. Remember that Mephibosheth was taken from Lo-debar, and now we find him dwelling in Jerusalem. What a difference—*Jerusalem* means one whom possesses peace.

I pray that no matter what has affected your life in a negative way, at our Lord's and King's table, you will find peace and grace and learn to live with a limp.

9

THE DISGUISE OF DECEPTION

Jesus warned his disciples to beware of deception. The Bible even tells us in the last days that many will be deceived. Before we look at several accounts of people who were deceived, let me define the word *deception*: the practice of misleading somebody. From the thesaurus, we find words like *dishonesty*, *trickery*, *sham*, and *fraud* to *con*.

No one wants to be taken advantage of. This form of deception comes from the enemy. Even as early as Genesis, we see the devil, called the serpent, deceiving Eve. Many of us know the story: God told Adam and Eve that they could eat from all the trees of the garden except for one—the one called the tree of knowledge of good and evil.

The account is in Genesis 2:16–18: "And the Lord *God* commanded the man, saying 'Of every tree of the garden thou mayest freely eat but of the tree of the knowledge of good and evil thou shalt not eat of it for in the day that thou eatest thereof thou shalt surely die'" (emphasis added).

The Bible even tells us that all the trees were pleasant to the sight, good for food and that the tree of life was in the middle of the garden (Gen. 2:9).

How different the outcome would have been if only the man and his wife had eaten from the tree of life before she was beguiled and deceived by the enemy. The New Testament makes it so clear that she was deceived and that she offered the fruit from this tree to Adam, and he ate it with her. Look at how the Bible describes what happened so long ago: "And Adam was not the one deceived; it was the woman who was deceived and became a sinner" (1 Tim. 2:14, NIV).

What Was It About This Tree?

The first deception happened in Genesis 3:1–6 (emphasis added):

> Now the serpent was more subtle than any beast of the field which the LORD *God* had made. And he said unto the woman "Yea, hath God said ye shall not eat of every tree of the garden?" And the woman said unto the serpent "we may eat of the fruit of the trees of the garden but of the fruit of the tree which is in the midst of the garden, God hath said, Ye shall not eat of it, neither shall ye touch it, lest ye die." And the serpent said unto the woman "Ye shall not surely die for God doth know that in the day ye eat thereof, then your eyes shall be opened and ye shall be as gods knowing good and evil." And when the

> woman saw that the tree was good for food and that it was pleasant to the eyes and a tree to be desired to make one wise; she took of the fruit thereof and did eat and gave unto her husband with her; and he did eat.

Notice how the enemy twisted the words of God. Satan said, "God said you may not eat of any of the trees." It went from the restriction of one tree to the enemy, telling her God said they can't eat of any of the trees that were good for food. This does not make sense to me that God would supply the food for them and then tease them by not allowing them to consume the very things he made to bless them.

One of the first mistakes the woman made was to engage in a conversation with the devil over the word of God. She then added her take on what He had told her by saying, "We are not even allowed to touch it, lest we die." God never said anything to her about touching it, but He did tell them that they would die.

Since all the trees were pleasant and good for food (Gen. 2:9), what was the difference that caused her to sin? I believe it was the phrase "to make one wise" that she ate and gave the fruit to her husband who was with her. We know the rest of the story of how man died spiritually, lost his walk with God, and was exiled from the garden. But thanks be to God that the last Adam came and was resurrected in a garden to give us the new birth, and we recovered thru him the fellowship lost through deception and disobedience.

Satan the Shape Shifter

Remember what the Bible teaches us about the wily ways of Satan! Our example here is from Paul writing to the Corinthians:

> And I will keep on doing what I am doing in order to cut the ground from under those who want an opportunity to be considered equal with us in the things they boast about. For such people are false apostles, deceitful workers, masquerading as apostles of Christ. And no wonder for Satan himself masquerades as an angel of light. It is not surprising then if his servants also masquerade as servants of righteousness. Their end will be what their actions deserve. (2 Cor. 11:12–15, NIV)

The New International Version uses the word *masquerading* and the King James says, "For such are false apostles, deceitful workers, *transforming* themselves into the apostles of Christ." The word *transformed* is defined as to change something dramatically, to undergo total change. Other related words to the word *transformed* are *altered*, *distorted*, and *misshapen*. Satan is a fallen angel, and he is the prince of darkness, so in order to mislead us, he changes his appearance into an angel of light.

The Bible said he masquerades as an angel of light. I am sure we have all heard of a masquerade party, where people change their appearance by wearing a costume or a mask. The word *masquerade* is defined as a pretense or a costume that disguises the true appearance.

Please Use Your Common Sense

One of the greatest deceptions in the Old Testament was when Jacob deceived his father, Isaac. There are several things we can learn from this account that can help with discernment so as not to be deceived. Genesis chapter 27 tells the story of a great deception.

> Isaac was old and his eyes were so weak that he could no longer see when he called for Esau his older son and said to him, "I am now an old man and don't know the day of my death. Get your equipment and go out to the open country to hunt some wild game for me. Then prepare me the kind of tasty food I like and bring it to me to eat so that I may give you my blessing before I die." Now Rebekah was listening as Isaac spoke to his son Esau. When Esau left for the open country to hunt game and bring it back, Rebekah said to her son Jacob "Look, I overheard your father say to your brother Esau 'Bring me some game and prepare me some tasty food to eat, so that I may give you my blessing in the presence of the LORD before I die.' Now, my son, listen carefully and do what I tell you: Go out to the

flock and bring me two choice young goats so I can prepare some tasty food for your father, just the way he likes it. Then take it to your father to eat, so that he may give you his blessing before he dies." Jacob said to his mother "But my brother Esau is a hairy man while I have smooth skin. What if my father touches me? I would appear to be tricking him and would bring down a curse on myself rather than a blessing." His mother said "My son, let the curse fall on me. Just do what I say; go and get them for me." So he went and got them and brought them to his mother and she prepared some tasty food just the way his father liked it. Then Rebekah took the best clothes of Esau her older son, which she had in the house and put them on her younger son Jacob. She also covered his hands and the smooth part of his neck with the goatskins. Then she handed to her son Jacob the tasty food and the bread she had made. He went to his father and said, "My father." "Yes, my son," he answered. "Who is it?" Jacob said to his father, "I am Esau your firstborn. I have done as you told me. Please sit up and eat some of my game, so that you may give me your blessing." Isaac asked his son, "How did you find it so quickly, my son?" "The LORD your God gave me success," he replied. Then Isaac said "Come near so I can touch you, my son, to know whether you really are my son Esau or not." Jacob went close to his father Isaac, who touched him and said "The voice is the voice of Jacob but the hands are the hands of Esau." He did not recognize him, for his hands were hairy like those of his brother Esau; so he proceeded to bless him. "Are you really my son Esau?" he asked "I am," he replied. Then he said, "My son, bring me some of your game to eat so that I may give you my blessing." Jacob brought it to him and he ate and he brought some wine and he drank. Then his father Isaac said to him, "Come here, my son, and kiss me." So he went to him and kissed him. When Isaac caught the smell of his clothes, he blessed him and said "Ah, the smell of my son is like the smell of a field that the LORD has blessed. (Gen. 27:1–27, NIV)

Notice that verse 5 says that Esau was Isaac's son, and then in verse 6, it says Jacob was Rebekah's son. Remember that these boys were twins, and from these statements, we can conclude that there was some favoritism shown, and this can divide children and families.

Let us start out with verse 12, where Jacob says, "What if my father touches me? I would appear to be tricking him and would bring down a curse on myself rather than a blessing." Interesting isn't it that he says "my father will feel me"? We have been taught in the church to not go by our feelings and that we live by faith and not by sight, however, when it comes to discernment, we must pay attention to our God-given feelings. Later on in this account in verse 21, Isaac asked his son to come near to him so he can feel him.

By Use and Exercise We Develop Discernment

In Hebrews 5:14, we read, "But solid food is for the mature, who by constant use have trained [their senses] to distinguish good from evil." This awesome verse tells us that by using our senses, we can discern first good, then evil. Not just evil; too many people want to look for evil, devils, demons, and on, but this ability from God is primarily to discern good.

My first point I want to make is do not be afraid to ask questions. In verse 18, Isaac asks, "Who are you my son?" And of course Jacob lies and says that he is Esau. Then Isaac asks another question, "How did you find it so quickly, my son?" Again Jacob lies and says the Lord brought this animal to him. Then yet again question number three is found in verse 24, "Are you really my son Esau?" Never fear asking questions because I believe that Isaac had a feeling that things just were right. If he didn't have some unrest, why so many questions?

The second thing to pay attention to is your feelings. In verse 21, Isaac asked his son to come near so that he may feel him. Remember that was Jacob's fear in verse 12—that his father would feel him. Please don't ignore your instincts when something just doesn't feel quite right. Pay attention.

The third thing is do not ignore the warnings. Look again at verse 22. He says the voice is Jacob's, but the hands are Esau's. Voices are very distinctive, and if it was Jacobs's voice, it is because it was Jacob's regardless of the hair that Rebekah put on his hands. The next verse is very sad because it says that Isaac did not discern him, and so he blessed him. The word *discerned* in verse 23 is defined as to scrutinize something. Let me define the word scrutinize—to observe somebody or something closely, to examine, and inspect, to analyze. Isaac did not do any of the above and, therefore, was deceived enough though he had been warned. And once again, he asked the same question, "Art thou my very son Esau?" (v. 24) *The fourth thing* that is of importance to us is our sense of smell. In verse 27, Isaac called his son near to not only kiss him but to smell his raiment. How does our smell help us in discernment? The answer to this question is found in Isaiah 11:1–3, where Jesus teaches us how to have the proper discernment.

> And there shall come forth a rod out of the stem of Jesse, and a Branch shall grow out of his roots: And the spirit of the LORD shall rest upon him, the spirit of wisdom and understanding, the spirit of counsel and might, the spirit of knowledge and of the fear of the LORD; And shall make him of *quick understanding* in the fear of the LORD: and he shall not judge after the sight of his eyes, neither reprove after the hearing of his ears. (emphasis added)

This verse tells us that Jesus did not judge by what he saw or heard; as a matter of fact, this scripture tells us that God's Spirit will make us quick to understand. When I did some research on this topic, I was amazed to learn that the word *quick understanding* in Hebrew is the word *smell*.

Interesting, isn't it, that Jacob was concerned that his father would smell him?

Have you ever met a person who looks right, talks right, acts right, yet something just doesn't smell quite right?

Don't be Fooled by Appearances

I want to explore one more very important story that will help us greatly. It is found in the book of Joshua, chapter 9. Joshua judged after the sight of his eyes and the hearing of his ear, and he made a huge mistake. My prayer is that this example will help us to avoid the same mistakes that he made.

> And it came to pass, when all the kings which were on this side Jordan, in the hills, and in the valleys, and in all the coasts of the great sea over against Lebanon, the Hittite, and the Amorite, the Canaanite, the Perizzite, the Hivite, and the Jebusite, heard thereof; That they gathered themselves together, to fight with Joshua and with Israel, with one accord. And when the inhabitants of Gibeon heard what Joshua had done unto Jericho and to Ai, They did work wilily, and went and made

as if they had been ambassadors, and took old sacks upon their asses, and wine bottles, old, and rent, and bound up; And old shoes and clouted upon their feet, and old garments upon them; and all the bread of their provision was dry and mouldy. And they went to Joshua unto the camp at Gilgal, and said unto him, and to the men of Israel, We be come from a far country: now therefore make ye a league with us. And the men of Israel said unto the Hivites, Peradventure ye dwell among us; and how shall we make a league with you? And they said unto Joshua, We are thy servants. And Joshua said unto them, Who are ye? and from whence come ye? And they said unto him, From a very far country thy servants are come because of the name of the LORD thy God: for we have heard the fame of him, and all that he did in Egypt, And all that he did to the two kings of the Amorites, that were beyond Jordan, to Sihon king of Heshbon, and to Og king of Bashan, which was at Ashtaroth. Wherefore our elders and all the inhabitants of our country spake to us, saying, Take victuals with you for the journey, and go to meet them, and say unto them, We are your servants: therefore now make ye a league with us. This our bread we took hot for our provision out of our houses on the day we came forth to go unto you; but now, behold, it is dry, and it is mouldy: And these bottles of wine, which we filled, were new; and, behold, they be rent: and these our garments and our shoes are become old by reason of the very long journey. And the men took of their victuals, and asked not counsel at the mouth of the LORD. And Joshua made peace with them, and made a league with them, to let them live: and the princes of the congregation sware unto them. And it came to pass at the end of three days after they had made a league with them, that they heard that they were their neighbours, and that they dwelt among them. And the children of Israel journeyed, and came unto their cities on the third day. Now their cities were Gibeon, and Chephirah, and Beeroth, and Kirjathjearim. And the children of Israel smote them not, because the princes of the congregation had sworn unto them by the LORD God of Israel. And all the congregation murmured against the princes. But all the princes said unto all the congregation, We have sworn unto them by the LORD God of Israel: now therefore we may not touch them. This we will do to them; we will even let them live, lest wrath be upon us, because of the oath which we sware unto them. And the princes said unto them, Let them live; but let them be hewers of wood and drawers of water unto all the congregation; as the princes had promised them. And Joshua called for them, and he spake unto them, saying, Wherefore have ye beguiled us, saying, We are very far from you; when ye dwell among us?

Before I get to the important aspect, there are some little things I want to point out. As the Gibeonites approach Joshua's men, the first thing they say is "we came from a far country, and the replay from the men of Israel is maybe you dwell near us? (vv. 6–7) Then in the next verse (8), "And Joshua asked them were have you come from?" And by the time we get to verse 9, they will add to their lie. Remember in verse 6 they said they came from a far country, but now in verse 9, it's a very far country. And finally, in verse 13, it becomes a very long journey.

Not only the children of Israel but Joshua himself are now asking questions. And they were lied to. How do we protect ourselves from deceptive people and lying spirits? By always seeking God's counsel from his word, from prayer, and from other people's insight.

The real problem in this account is not the Gibeonites, nor their disguise, nor their lying. The true downfall in this story is verse 14: "They asked not counsel at the mouth of the Lord." Here are some other versions for clarity. "The Israelites sampled their provisions but did not inquire of the LORD" (New International Version). "The men of Israel looked them over and accepted the evidence. But they didn't ask GOD about it" (The Message).

We must always seek God and listen to the voice of His Spirit. I want to share three scriptures that have been very helpful to me in growing in discernment. I believe we can avoid deception if we apply these three principles to our lives.

How to Develop Discernment

Primarily, we discern by the scriptures; second, by the spirit; and third, by our senses.

"For the word of God is quick, and powerful, and sharper than any two-edged sword, piercing even to the dividing asunder of soul and spirit, and of the joints and marrow, and is a *discerner* of the thoughts and intents of the heart" (Hebrews 4:12; emphasis added) Always remember that we are three parts—spirit, soul, and body (1 Thess 5:23)—and from the above scripture, we see that God's Word will help us discern all three. We see a division between soul and spirit, and then the joints and marrow, which speak of our bodies.

We must know God's word and God's spirit. One of the gifts of the Holy Spirit is discerning of spirits.

"To another the working of miracles; to another prophecy; to another discerning of spirits; to another divers kinds of tongues; to another the interpretation of tongues" (1 Corinthians 12:10). When we look at the gifts of the spirit even in the verse above, we notice that it is not discerning of spirit but discerning of spirits in plural. What is it we must discern?

With God's help, we are to discern between the human spirit, evil spirits, and God's spirit.

In addition, I have found Hebrews 5:14 to be a great help: "But strong meat belongeth to them that are of full age, even those who by reason of use have their senses exercised to discern both good and evil."

Please notice that because of the use of our senses, we discern good from evil, not evil from good.

God told Ezekiel that the priest's were to teach this to God's people: "And they shall teach my people the difference between the holy and profane, and cause them to discern between the unclean and the clean" (Ezekiel 44:23). Moreover, when the Lord appeared to Solomon and told him he could ask for anything, Solomon requested discernment. Look at how this request pleased the Lord.

> In Gibeon the LORD appeared to Solomon in a dream by night: and God said, Ask what I shall give thee. And Solomon said, Thou hast shewed unto thy servant David my father great mercy, according as he walked before thee in truth, and in righteousness, and in uprightness of heart with thee; and thou hast kept for him this great kindness, that thou hast given him a son to sit on his throne, as it is this day. And now, O LORD my God, thou hast made thy servant king instead of David my father: and I am but a little child: I know not how to go out or come in. And thy servant is in the midst of thy people which thou hast chosen, a great people, that cannot be numbered nor counted for multitude. Give therefore thy servant an understanding heart to judge thy people, that I may *discern between good and bad*: for who is able to judge this thy so great

a people? And the speech pleased the LORD, that Solomon had asked this thing. (1 Samuel 3:5–10; emphasis added)

May each of us stay in the word of God as it will discern the thought and the intents of the heart, and I pray that we will pay attention to our God-given senses and that the Holy Spirit would help us discern as we seek counsel from God. Then we will not be deceived, and we can heed the warnings of Jesus. "Behold, I send you forth as sheep in the midst of wolves: be ye therefore wise as serpents, and harmless as doves" (Matthew 10:16).

10

HOW TO BE A GIANT KILLER

The most famous story in the Bible is about a giant David slew named Goliath. Even people who do not read the scriptures have heard this story. I want to make several key points that will help us to bring down the giants in our lives. First, let us do a refresher and look at 1 Samuel chapter 17.

> Now the Philistines gathered together their armies to battle, and were gathered together at Shochoh, which belongeth to Judah and pitched between Shochoh and Azekah, in Ephesdammim. And Saul and the men of Israel were gathered together and pitched by the valley of Elah and set the battle in array against the Philistines. And the Philistines stood on a mountain on the one side, and Israel stood on a mountain on the other side: and there was a valley between them. (1 Sam. 17:1–3, KJV)

Are You a Philistine?

It is of importance for us to make sure that we are not Philistines when we set out to tackle the giants in our lives. The word *Philistine* means "to roll in the dust and to wallow in self." Ouch, that hurts because there have been many times in my life that I allowed self-pity and ended up wallowing in self. You can see from the above scripture that the battle took place in the valley of Elah. The word for valley in this verse is *depression* and the definition for Elah is stronghold. The one giant that must be subdued in all of our lives is depression, which can become a stronghold.

Who is Goliath?

> And there went out a champion out of the camp of the Philistines, named Goliath, of Gath, whose height was six cubits and a span. And he had a helmet of brass upon his head and he was armed with a coat of mail; and the weight of the coat was five thousand shekels of brass (about one hundred twenty-five pounds). And he had greaves of brass upon his legs and a target of brass between his shoulders. And the staff of his spear was like a weaver's beam; and his spear's head weighed six hundred shekels of iron: and one bearing a shield went before him. (1 Sam. 17:4–6)

The name Goliath means "to exile, take captive, to strip." The enemy's plan is to try and exile us, which is defined as unwilling absence from a place of residence, banishment, to deport as refugee or outcast.

Goliath came from Gath. The word *Gath* is a "winepress." Giants or issues of great heaviness can cause us to feel pressed and crushed. In addition, the plan of the enemy is to separate us from one another and make us feel alone as an outcast. However, thanks be to God for Jesus and the body of Christ, we are never alone.

The Scent of Fear

> And he stood and cried unto the armies of Israel and said unto them "Why are ye come out to set your battle in array? Am not I a Philistine and ye servants to Saul? Choose you a man for you, and let him come down to me. If he be able to fight with me and to kill me then will we be your servants but if I prevail against him and kill him then shall ye be our servants, and serve us." And the Philistine said "I defy the armies of Israel this day; give me a man, that we may fight together." When Saul and all Israel heard those words of the Philistine; they were dismayed, and greatly afraid. Now David was the son of that Ephrathite of Bethlehem Judah, whose name was Jesse and he had eight sons: and the man went among men for an old man in the days of Saul. And the three eldest sons of Jesse went and followed Saul to the battle: and the names of his three sons that went to the battle were Eliab the firstborn and next unto him Abinadab and the third

> Shammah. And David was the youngest: and the three eldest followed Saul. (1 Sam.17:8–14)

Please note: the men of Israel who were all dressed for battle may have looked fierce on the outside, but inside they are filled with fear. As the King James Version puts it, they were dismayed and greatly afraid. Let me define the word *dismayed—to be shattered and broken*; and they were *greatly afraid* means to be *terrified and to dread*.

Before we are able to conquer any issue or giant in our lives, we first must deal with our fears, especially the ones on the inside of us. The enemy moves in on us when we have hidden fears. If we do not take them to the Lord, they can grow and fester inside of us until that spirit of fear has a stronghold in our lives. We need to remember that fear is not from God, and He wants us to have a spirit of power, love, and a sound mind. Thank God for 2 Timothy 1:7: "For God hath not given us the spirit of fear; but of power, and of love, and of a sound mind."

First and Foremost is Obedience

> But David went and returned from Saul to feed his father's sheep at Bethlehem. And the Philistine drew near morning and evening, and presented himself forty days. And Jesse said unto David his son "Take now for thy brethren an ephah of this parched corn and these ten loaves and run to the camp of thy brethren. And carry these ten cheeses

unto the captain of their thousand, and look how thy brethren fare and take their pledge. Now Saul, and they and all the men of Israel were in the valley of Elah fighting with the Philistines. And David rose up early in the morning and left the sheep with a keeper and took and went as Jesse had commanded him and he came to the trench as the host was going forth to the fight, and shouted for the battle. (1 Sam. 17:15–20)

David's father, Jesse, told him to take some food to his older brothers. Did you notice the phrases "David rose up early in the morning and as Jesse had commanded"? The spiritual application here is that David obeyed his father's commandment. Whenever we are engaged in a battle, the first thing that is of key importance is that we are in obedience to our father's commandments.

God has promised to defend us and give us the land where the giants dwell, but it is our responsibility to obey God's word and follow his commandments.

One of my favorite verses in the Bible deals with the act of obedience. It's Acts 5:32: "God gives the Holy Spirit to those who obey Him." The Word of God tells us that God prefers obedience over sacrifice. Sometimes to obey takes a real sacrifice on our part, but when we obey, we will have an increase in the anointing of the Holy Spirit.

David approaches the battlefield and overhears the threat coming from the enemy. He inquires as to what will be done for the man who defeats this giant. They tell him that whoever can silence this champion will be given great riches and become one of King Saul's sons-in-law and that all of his family will be tax-exempt forever. Wow, the one I like most is the thought of beings tax-exempt for life. Can you even image never owing or paying taxes?

Second Important Step

We must overcome the opinions of others even when it comes to our own family members.

> And Eliab his eldest brother heard when he spake unto the men and Eliab's anger was kindled against David, and he said "Why comest thou down hither? And with whom did you leave those few sheep in the wilderness? I know thy pride and the naughtiness of thine heart: for thou are come down that thou mightest see the battle." And David said, "What have I now done?" (1 Sam. 17:28–29)

Eliab, David's older brother, had it all wrong. There was no pride or arrogance in David coming to the battlefield. As a matter of fact, Eliab insulted David when he made the remark about the few sheeps in the field. When you criticize a man's work, you have done him an injustice.

I think that maybe Eliab resented that David was chosen over him to be the king. Remember when Samuel came to the house of Jesse to anoint the next king (1 Sam. 16) and David was chosen over all of his brothers. Eliab was the firstborn and should have been chosen. Maybe he had a spirit of entitlement. Another reason may have been that he himself did nothing to stop the torments of the enemy.

So many times in our lives we look to our older believers for direction when what we really need to do is keep our focus on the Lord and his word. Many times, God will use the weakness among us to do His greatest work. After all, David was just a shepherd, and the Bible said that Eliab and his brothers were men of war and fully dressed for the battle.

Lord, help us to overcome rejection or criticism from those closest to us. Our own family members don't always understand what God is doing or what our assignment is, but we must be obedient and not let a lack of support stop us from moving forward.

Third is Your Competency Will Be Challenged

Word reached King Saul that David was ready to get the nation of Israel a victory over this uncircumcised Philistine. Look at the king's reaction to this pertinent information in 1 Samuel 17:32–33: "David said to Saul 'Let no one lose heart on account of this Philistine; your servant will go and fight him.' Saul replied 'You are not able to go out against this Philistine and fight him you are only a young man and he has been a warrior from his youth.'"

Have you ever heard the words "you are not able"? For many years, this was an ongoing battle for me. The enemy would remind me of all my weakness, and over and over again I had to fight this one little phrase—"you are not able."

I would try to muster faith to overcome this attack, but in the bottom of my heart, I knew that there was a grain of truth in this statement. After several defeats, I was crying and praying to the Lord to help me overcome this lingering problem. What He said was shocking: He told me, "Agree quickly with my adversity."

The next time the enemy brought up my lack of ability instead of battling with rebuttals, I simply said, "Yes I am not able. *However*, greater is He who's in me, and it is God who works and wills to do his good pleasure in me. So when I am weak, then He is strong." Finally, this was put to rest because we all need God to enable us to fulfill His calling in our lives, and we must depend on Him for each battle and know that our sufficiency comes from Him and not from ourselves.

Fourth: Do You Have the Correct Armor?

After David assured King Saul that he was totally dependent on God for the victory, King Saul did something unusual. He called for David and proceeded to equip him with his armor. Remember that Saul was head and shoulders taller than any of the other men. In my mind, he is a 56 long and David is a 38 regular. Can you picture this in your mind a six-foot-two man and a five-foot-six man standing next to each other?

"Then Saul dressed David in his own tunic. He put a coat of armor on him and a bronze helmet on his head. David fastened on his sword over the tunic and tried walking around, because he was not used to them. 'I cannot go in these,' he said to Saul 'because I am not used to them.' So he took them off." (1 Sam 17:38–39)

What an important lesson we each need to learn that we can never wear someone else's armor.

Many years ago, I was teaching at a women's conference in the Virgin Islands, and another woman was speaking, and she asked the question if anyone knew the armor of God. I quickly raised my hand, and she asked me to stand, and when I did, I began to recite the armor of God—belt, shoes, breastplate, helmet, sword, and shield. What happened next was hard to understand at the moment. She told me I was incorrect and to please be seated.

Well, I sat down all right. You could see the smoke coming out of my nostrils. What did she mean I was incorrect? I know the scripture in Ephesians chapter 6. She then said something that has been life-changing for me. We were warned not to make the symbol the substance. The symbol of the armor of God is a belt, but that is not the substance; the substance is truth, which is the first piece of the armor.

The second symbol is a breastplate, but the armor is righteousness. Then we have our feet shod with peace; next we see a shield, but the armor is faith; next we see a helmet, but once again, the substance is salvation, not the symbol of a helmet. The sword is the Word of God.

As long as I live, I will be indebted to this wonderful sister and never forget this great statement: don't make the symbol the substance.

How do we wear the armor of others? Pretty simple, when we hear that someone is getting up early in the morning to pray and that they have seen amazing things begin to happen. All of a sudden, we want to get up early and pray. Please understand, early morning prayer is wonderful; but sometimes, we are just copying what others are doing—the same with Bible reading, fasting, and speaking the word of God along with meditation. All these are right and good things to do, but when we try to move in someone else's armor that we haven't tested, it will not have the same effect it has for them because this was their assignment.

David said I cannot wear this armor. I have not proved it. God has just the right fit for each of us, whether we are tall or short, male or female, thin or heavy, young or old. How I praise the Lord for the truth, righteousness, peace, faith, salvation, and the Word of God.

Remember Our Covenant

When you read through this chapter, you will notice that David never calls Goliath by name. He only calls him an uncircumcised Philistine. What David is implying is that Goliath has no blood covenant with God. In the Bible, you would circumcise a baby boy at the time you dedicated him to the Lord, and then He would receive his name. John the Baptist as well as Jesus both received their name at their circumcision.

Speaking of names, this was one of the powerful weapons that David used to bring down this giant in 1 Samuel 17:45: "Then said David to the Philistine 'Thou comest to me with a sword, and with a spear and with a shield but I come to thee in the name of the LORD of hosts, the God of the armies of Israel, whom thou hast defied.'" Always remember in your battles to call on the name of the Lord. Look at what He has promised us when we call on him.

> The name of the LORD is a strong tower: the righteous runneth into it and is safe. (Proverbs 18:10)

> Then called I upon the name of the LORD; O LORD, I beseech thee, deliver my soul. (Psalm 116:4)

> Nations compassed me about but in the name of the LORD will I destroy them. They compassed me about; yea, they compassed me about: but in the name of the LORD I will destroy them. They compassed me about like bees: they are quenched as the fire of thorns: for in the name of the LORD I will destroy them. (Psalm 118:10–12)

> Our help is in the name of the LORD, who made heaven and earth. (Psalm124:8)

As David approached his enemy, he remembered that it was the name of the Lord, and it was God's battle.

> This day will the LORD deliver thee into mine hand
> and I will smite thee and take thine head from
> thee and I will give the carcass of the host of the
> Philistines this day unto the fowls of the air and
> to the wild beasts of the earth; that all the earth
> may know that there is a God in Israel. And all this
> assembly shall know that the LORD saves not with
> sword and spear: for the battle is the LORD's and he
> will give you into our hands. (1 Sam. 17:46–47)

David took his stone and his slingshot and fired away, and down came the ten-foot-tall giant. David then took Goliath's sword and cut off his head. (I was teaching at a youth retreat, and I wanted to teach on this portion of scripture, and I needed something catching that would engage the kids. So I titled my message "How to get ahead in life".)

If we will follow these simple truths that no matter what we are fighting, when we walk in obedience to our father's commands, learning how to overcome the rejection or disapproval of others, never forgetting that all our sufficiency and competence comes for God, He has provided the perfect armor—handpicked and designed for each of us. As we take His name into each battle, knowing we are covered by his blood, we are assured of the victory, and each of us can get ahead in life.

CPSIA information can be obtained at www.ICGtesting.com
Printed in the USA
BVOW02s2132180916

462179BV00010B/4/P